Naming GOD

Naming GOD

Selected Readings Representing Differing Perspectives

EDITED BY
CELIA WOLF-DEVINE

A Herder & Herder Book
THE CROSSROAD PUBLISHING COMPANY
NEW YORK

A Herder & Herder Book
The Crossroad Publishing Company www.crossroadpublishing.com

© 2019 by Celia Wolf-Devine

Crossroad, Herder & Herder, and the crossed C logo/colophon are registered trademarks of The Crossroad Publishing Company.

All rights reserved. No part of this book may be copied, scanned, reproduced in any way, or stored in a retrieval system, or transmitted, in any form or by any means, electronic, mechanical, photocopying, recording, or otherwise, without the written permission of The Crossroad Publishing Company. For permission please write to rights@crossroadpublishing.com.

In continuation of our 200-year tradition of independent publishing, The Crossroad Publishing Company proudly offers a variety of books with strong, original voices and diverse perspectives. The viewpoints expressed in our books are not necessarily those of The Crossroad Publishing Company, any of its imprints or of its employees, executives, owners. Although the author and publisher have made every effort to ensure that the information in this book was correct at press time, the author and publisher do not assume and hereby disclaim any liability to any party for any loss, damage, or disruption caused by errors or omissions, whether such errors or omissions result from negligence, accident, or any other cause. No claims are made or responsibility assumed for any health or other benefits.

The text of this book is set in 11/16 Garamond MT Pro.

Composition by Sophie Appel
Cover design by Sophie Appel

Library of Congress Cataloging-in-Publication Data
available upon request from the Library of Congress.

ISBN 978-0-8245-5040-0 paperback
ISBN 978-0-8245-5039-4 cloth
ISBN 978-0-8245-5043-1 ePub
ISBN 978-0-8245-5044-8 mobi

Books published by The Crossroad Publishing Company may be purchased at special quantity discount rates for classes and institutional use. For information, please e-mail sales@crossroadpublishing.com.

CONTENTS

Acknowledgments   vii
Preface   ix

Introduction: Naming the Supreme Being   1

**The Sacredness of Nature and Cosmic Religion:
Sky Gods and Mother Earth**   13
MIRCEA ELIADE

Genesis: Chapters 1–3   21

**Why Women Need the Goddess:
Phenomenological, Psychological, and Political Reflections**   27
CAROL P. CHRIST

Basic Linguistic Options: God, Women, Equivalence …   37
ELIZABETH JOHNSON

On the Fatherhood of God   47
JULI LOESCH WILEY

Is "God the Mother" Just as Good?   51
JULI LOESCH WILEY

In Defense of the Male Priesthood   57
JULI LOESCH WILEY

Making Inclusive Language Inclusive: A Christian Gay Man's View   63
RICHARD DAVIS

God the Father, God the Mother, and Goddesses   69
SUSANNE HEINE

Why Christians Name God "Father"   81
GARY CULPEPPER

Ecofeminism: Symbolic and Social Connections of the Oppression of Women and the Domination of Nature   89
ROSEMARY RADFORD RUETHER

Women in Genesis 1–3   101
EDITH BLACK

Traditional Judaism and Feminine Spirituality   109
TAMAR FRANKIEL

Difference Feminism and the Role of Women in the Church   121
CELIA WOLF-DEVINE

For Further Reading   131
About the Contributors   135

ACKNOWLEDGMENTS

I wish to express my special gratitude to Philip Devine, with whom I co-edited the 2003 book. He was helpful at every level during the time we worked on it, and was especially good at writing probing questions for reflection after each reading.

In putting together this revised version of the material on naming the supreme being, I am deeply indebted to Professor Gary Culpepper, chair of the Theology Department at Providence College, for taking an interest in this project and talking out ideas with me. His encouragement and support were a great help. He and his graduate assistant, Bridget Scott, helped by doing a literature search to ascertain what competing books were out there, and by obtaining permission to reprint the selections.

I am also grateful to Chris Myers, the Crossroad editor in charge of this volume, for shepherding the project through the process of preparation for publication.

PREFACE

Issues connected with sex and gender are, in the contemporary world, deeply contested. Polarization has increased to such a degree that people are often both unwilling and unable to talk to each other. And this is the case in the religious world as well. Male and female and masculine and feminine are categories that ordinarily structure our thought—both in our daily encounters with each other and when we reflect about the reality that transcends our experience. This goes very deep in our religious history and enters into most of the world's religions; it is not unique to the major monotheistic religions (consider, for example, the concepts of *yang* and *yin* in Taoism). Within the Christian community, the practice of calling God "Father" has recently been strongly criticized by some theologians, and passions run high.

Some of the most extreme reactions against calling God "Father" rest on a confusion between sex and gender. Those who speak of God as "Father" are not asserting that God has a male body or organs, since God has no body. Sexual difference is biological, a matter of organs and chromosomes. But gender is a matter of social psychology, and renderings of the masculine-feminine distinction are as various as are individuals and the societies to which they belong. Gender presupposes sex, since it is what we make of our sexual differences, not of our height, ancestry, or talents. These categories come into play in our ordinary social interactions, but when we think about God, things become complicated. Thinking of God as personal invites us to think of God in terms of gender. When we think of God as the source of our being, parental imagery comes naturally, and this can stir up the deep and sometimes conflicted feelings people have about their own parents.

And the ramifications of thinking about God in gendered terms are broader than the implications of parental imagery. How we think about and imagine God and the language we use to refer to God are profoundly important to our religious lives at every level. God does not merely play an important role in the believer's intellectual understanding of reality. Our relationship with God also has an erotic dimension that needs to be taken into account pastorally. There is a deep connection between the sexual impulse and our religious yearnings; both are rooted in a deep restlessness, loneliness, and sense of incompleteness that we feel. We long for union with another who will make us whole and satisfy the hunger of our hearts. And our most intimate religious experiences cannot but be affected by our imaginative images of God.

The Bible includes a variety of images of God, both masculine (e.g., warrior, king) and feminine (e.g., a mother bird, or nursing mother) as well as inanimate images like "rock." Christians, however, have traditionally given special priority to "Father," because the Lord's Prayer, which Jesus instructed us to pray, begins with "Our Father."

Unfortunately, decisions about applying gendered language to the deity are sometimes constrained by editorial policies or else made in response to a vague but pervasive feeling of pressure to eliminate masculine pronouns. What seems to have disappeared is space to reflect about and rationally discuss why changes in traditional language are or are not appropriate. The essays in this volume present the most important arguments for and against calling God "Father" and invite the reader to reflect on the deeper issues underlying the way we apply gendered language to God and its implications. A variety of perspectives is included in order to get beyond polarization and provide a more complex and nuanced picture of the theological and pastoral issues involved.

These readings are a revised version of the final unit in *Sex and Gender: A Spectrum of Views*, edited by myself and Philip Devine and published by Wadsworth in 2003. It was our intention to promote reflection about sex and gender issues and to get away from an adversarial "us versus them" approach by presenting a variety of perspectives, looking at the reasons offered by each and trying to bring them into dialogue. The book evolved out of material I brought together for my students at Stonehill College. I taught a course entitled "Philosophy of Sex and Gender" for a number of years, and I found the book very successful in stimulating lively and open dialogue. It started with a discussion of reason and emotion and moved through units devoted to male/female difference, sexuality, reproduction, family, and gender in the political arena, concluding with the way gender structures our understanding of that reality which transcends our experience. The final unit was my special favorite, and the students enjoyed it because I had been able to locate some good, lively, and jargon-free essays that drew them into the discussion, in addition to those well-known authors whose work has been most influential in academic circles.

In order to bring order into the welter of different understandings of sexuality and sexual difference, Dr. Devine and I articulated four basic underlying worldviews that are operative in current debates, even when not stated explicitly. A quick explanation of them will help situate the selections in this book, and the reader is invited to try to discern the different worldviews at work under the surface in the readings. For, although the authors whose work is reprinted here are almost all working within, or reacting against, a traditional Christian framework, Christianity has always existed in a world where believers are surrounded by people with competing ways of thinking, and these have often bled into the Christian tradition. According to the Jewish and Christian view of nature, the created world is good, and our embodiment is good. God created human beings male and female. Sexuality is not itself divine, but participates in sacredness because sexual intercourse was ordained by God, and because through it we can cooperate with God in the generation of new human beings (*Genesis* 1:28; 4:1; 9:7). Within the Jewish and Christian traditions, current controversies center upon what we are to make of sex difference—does it imply differing roles for men and women, either in the rituals and practices of their religion, or in the broader society?

A second worldview that has come on the scene fairly recently is naturalism, which strips the world of all spiritual or supernatural powers. The world is only what science tells us it is. This emerged out of the Scientific Revolution of the seventeenth century, when the science in question was mechanistic physics, but scientific explanations of nature have of course developed and branched out into a multitude of sophisticated disciplines such as biochemistry and genetics. Contemporary naturalists tend to regard sex as a normal, healthy human function, like the need to eat. It can be conducive to intimacy between people, but needs to be governed rationally. Naturalists differ on the question of what we are to make of sexual difference. Some regard it as simply a biological fact we have to live with, but since there are no norms or purposes to constrain us, others leave the door open to various surgical and hormonal interventions designed to make a person's body as much like the sex/gender he or she prefers as possible. Nature, however, has laws independent of our will, and our interventions, therefore, may have unexpected and unwelcome consequences.

Two competing, and broadly religious, worldviews that have been historically very important and that remain influential are paganism and Manichaeanism. Paganism, which is currently experiencing something of a revival (among goddess worshipers and neo-Odinists, for example), holds that there are a number of gods or divine beings who can and do come into conflict. Sexuality manifests the operation of powerful deities. Thus, for example, the behavior of Helen of Troy (whose adultery was the cause of the Trojan War) was explained by saying that she had been taken over by Aphrodite (the goddess of sex). Being considered sacred, then, the power of sexuality is regarded with awe and surrounded with rituals and taboos.

Manichaeanism holds that the physical world (including the body) is bad, having been created not by an all good and all powerful God, but by an inferior and possibly evil spiritual being. The spirit is good, and the flesh is bad. So sex is either spiritualized or regarded as degrading—a view that has often been influential upon (and sometimes even confused with) the Christian tradition. Reproduction is regarded with special horror because it traps another soul in the muck and mire of the physical world. Hostility to reproduction is common these days, and this can be indicative of an underlying Manichaean tendency.

This book is unique and fills an important gap in the literature. There are other books that address the question of naming the Supreme Being, but none of them collect competing perspectives on the question. Most are written by a single author and present the issue from a single point of view. A few present the work of several authors, but the authors are all representative of one particular approach. This collection is intended for undergraduate and graduate students in theology or religious studies programs. Seminarians and liturgists will profit from it, and those who teach Philosophy of Religion may find that it stimulates their students because it carries them beyond the well-worn arguments for or against the existence of God into questions about how we conceive of and imagine that deity.

Each selection is followed by questions for reflection. A bibliography with suggestions for further reading makes this book appropriate for nonspecialist readers who are interested in the question as currently debated among scholars in the Jewish and Christian traditions.

INTRODUCTION

Naming the Supreme Being

Sexuality has cosmic significance for a number of reasons. On an individual level, there is a deep similarity between the sexual impulse and the religious impulse; both are connected with a sense of one's own incompleteness and a longing for wholeness. Thus, mystics in many traditions have recourse to sexual metaphors to describe the soul's union with God, and lovers often employ religious imagery in their poems. Aristophanes, in Plato's *Symposium*, explains all sexual desire by the hypothesis that there were once globular creatures with four arms, four legs, and two faces who were sliced in half by Zeus, leaving each half "with a desperate yearning for the other," so that when we are "longing after and following after that primeval wholeness, we say we are in love." And Augustine, addressing God, exclaims: "Thou has made us for Thyself, and our hearts are restless until they find rest in Thee."

The struggle over sex and gender issues, then, is not limited to the relationships individuals have with each other, nor even to questions about what sorts of social structures we should set up; it also extends to questions about the nature of Ultimate Reality. There has been a recurrent tendency in the religious history of humankind to think of Ultimate Reality in ways structured by the concepts of male and female, masculine and feminine, father and mother. This is the case even for religions that do not believe in a personal god. Taoists, for example, regard the *yang* and *yin* principles as fundamental to the deep structure of reality, and see them as complementary. *Yang* is hot, dry, active, light, and masculine, while *yin* is cold, moist, passive, dark, and feminine. *Yang* is movement; *yin* is rest.

As Eliade points out, "For religious man, nature is never only 'natural'; it is always fraught with a religious value." Being viewed as the handiwork of the gods, the world is taken to reveal various modalities of the sacred. Contemplation of the sky reveals transcendence, infinity, eternity, and a kind of absolute existence. The gods of many primitive people are called by names designating height—the "sky dweller," the "most high." Such gods are thought of in masculine terms such as "Lord," "Chief," or "Father." The sacredness of the Earth, by contrast, spontaneously reveals itself as *Terra Mater* (Mother Earth), universal genetrix who gives birth to all things. The sacrality of women (their magico-religious prestige), then, depends on the holiness of the earth, and feminine fecundity has a cosmic model in Mother Earth. Some religions regard the Cosmic Mother as capable of conceiving alone, while others believe that creation results from a sacred marriage between the Sky God and Mother Earth. Human marriage would, in this latter view, be viewed as a kind of imitation of the cosmic marriage. "I am Heaven . . . thou art Earth!" the husband proclaims in a Hindu wedding ritual. And ritual orgies in the fields, as practiced in some Ancient Near Eastern religions, might be expected by a kind of sympathetic magic to increase the fertility of the soil.

The use of parental imagery to refer to God is a recurrent pattern in human religious history also because so many of the world's religions see the world as the creation of God (or the gods), and it is through our parents that we receive life. God has no body, and thus any application of sexual imagery to God is not strictly literal. Some Mormon communities have taught that God the father has a physical body, but they are unique among American religious communities. But it does seem that the language we use in talking about God is important. The readings in this volume focus on the problem of naming the Supreme Being in monotheistic religions. (Polytheistic or nontheistic religions raise a different set of problems.) In choosing what language should be used to refer to God, it is helpful to look at the differing connotations of the terms *father* and *mother* first in a purely naturalistic context.

Differing Natural Connotations of the Terms "Father" and "Mother"

Differing Roles in Reproduction

Since the roles of the father and mother in reproduction are so dissimilar, calling God "Father" conveys very different things from calling God "Mother." The father is necessarily active; his act initiates the process of reproduction. Hence, as Wiley points out, paternal imagery emphasizes God's activity in creation. The child develops within the mother's body, tied to her by the umbilical cord, and literally takes his or her physical substance from the mother. To think of the source of our being as "Mother" thus conjures up images of immanence; we are somehow within the mother or continuous with her. To think of the source of our being as "father," by contrast, emphasizes the mysteriousness, remoteness, and transcendence of God; He initiates the process, but remains outside it. Who someone's mother is is never in doubt, whereas paternity can be unknown (and some nineteenth-century anthropologists supposed that entire cultures were ignorant of the biological facts of paternity). These sorts of associations with the word *father*, then, reinforce the connection between thinking of God as "Father" and the notion of transcendence, which Eliade discovered in so many cosmic religions.

Differences in the Infant's Relationship with Father and Mother

Finally, still reflecting about the notion of "God the Father" independently of particular religious traditions and their revealed scriptures, Freudians have claimed that children experience maternal power and paternal power very differently, and this means that thinking of God as Father will have very different emotional and cognitive resonances from thinking of God as Mother. The infant perceives Mother as an enormously powerful person, feels helplessly dependent on her for nourishment and care, and experiences a pull toward a dissolution of the self back into the mother (hence the association of the mother with dissolution and death as well as with nurturing and life manifested, for example, in the Hindu cult of Kali, the dark goddess who wears a necklace of skulls and drinks blood). Paternal power is experienced as more remote; Father sets limits and lays down rules for us to follow. While Mother may always be ready to forgive and shelter us, Father holds us accountable for our actions. He thus calls us out of a regressive over-identification with Mother and into objectivity and responsibility. This association of the father with authority and judgment is connected to Freud's suggestion that the father is associated with what he calls the "reality principle." As a result of Freud's association between the father and the reality principle, those in the Freudian tradition are likely to see in "God the Father" the principle that limits our pursuit of gratification—the objective reality that stands over and against us and our desires.

God the Father in Revelation

Those Americans who are religious are mainly Jewish, Christian, or Muslim. Revelation as understood in these traditions is connected with nature in complex ways. It takes up already existing natural imagery and symbolism, but it also builds on it and adds new levels of meaning. The very notion of revelation presupposes a God who breaks into history "from a place beyond the natural order of things" (to use Tamar Frankiel's phrase). Much of the debate in America has focused on how we should think of the one Supreme Being—for example, on whether or not Christians should call God "Father," and on the implications this has for the role of women (both within religious institutions and in society at large).

If we look at the scriptures of the three major monotheistic religions, we find that God is referred to using primarily (although not exclusively) masculine imagery. In the Hebrew scriptures, terms are used that imply majesty, dominion, and kingship. He is described as a mighty warrior, or as "Lord of Hosts," for example. Jesus teaches his disciples to call God "Father" in the "Lord's Prayer" recited by Christians everywhere. In Genesis 1–3, where pronouns are used to refer to God, they are masculine. The centrality of the male-female distinction to the created order is also clearly conveyed by Genesis 1:27, which says "male and female he created them." Allah, likewise, is thought of in strongly masculine terms. Differing and complementary sex roles for men and women in Jewish, Christian, and Muslim cultures have roots in their sacred scriptures. There are already hints of differing roles for men and women in the passage from Genesis, reprinted here, both in the meaning of the names given to Adam and Eve (as Edith Black points out), and in the different forms of punishment to which Adam and Eve are subject after the Fall. For Muslims, different roles for men and women are clearly set out in the divine law, which is based on the *Koran* and the *Hadith,* and Jewish religious law assigns certain important duties specifically to women and others to men.

Philosophical and Cultural Background to the Current Debate

Atheistic Projection Theories

For centuries, theologians and philosophers have puzzled over how human language can possibly describe the mysterious and transcendent God of faith, but in the twentieth century, discussion about religious language took on a new character. It is not just that human language is thought inadequate to describe God; rather, "God" has come to be viewed by many people as *only* a human creation—a kind of projection of human ideals or hopes onto the void (or onto chaos).

The most important sources of this type of projection theory were Marx, Nietzsche, and Freud. All three were atheists and attempted to account for the origins of people's belief in a "God" in naturalistic terms. They understood the nature of the projection mechanism involved somewhat differently, but for all of them, God is understood as a kind of human creation. Freud, for example, thought that we project into the Heavens our infantile image of the all-powerful father who loves and protects us because the harshness of reality is too hard to bear (the "religion as crutch" view). Marx, following Feuerbach, thought that "God" was a kind of projection of the ideal human essence that we project onto God because oppressive social institutions make it impossible to realize the fullness of our human essence here below. For Nietzsche, all systems of thought, including religion, were projections onto the Abyss undertaken by people whose will to power is very strong. Ideally, these would be superior people called *Übermenschen,* who create "new values" in full consciousness of their arbitrary character. But in the case of Judaism and Christianity, they have been members of a priestly class whose will to power is expressed in a way filled with resentment. But the projection of God and an eternal realm of forms established by our spiritual forbearers has failed, and we (or, rather, the most perceptive and spiritually potent among us) are now faced with the task of creating "new values." (This is the meaning of Nietzsche's notorious claim that God is dead.)

The Politicization of Language

Another important development in the twentieth century was the intense politicization of language. Philosophers became increasingly aware of the role of language in shaping our thought (in the analytic tradition, for example, through the influence of Wittgenstein, and in the continental tradition, for example, in the work of Derrida). On a more popular level, advertisers, politicians, and the media generally became very delicately attuned to the ways in which the language we use to describe something affects the way people will respond to it. Many people, therefore, sought to modify people's behavior and ways of thinking by trying to get them to use certain words and not others. Calling people "senior citizens" instead of "old" or "elderly," for example, would, they hoped, engender in us a more respectful attitude toward them, and gender-neutral or inclusive language was advocated as a way of combating sexist ways of thinking. So those who accepted the view that "God" is a human creation—if they did not simply reject religion as Freud, Marx, and Nietzsche did—often viewed the question of what language we should use to talk about God as a political choice to be made on the basis of which one would most effectively advance social movements of which they approved, such as feminism or the ecological movement.

Disputes about what language we should use to refer to God, therefore, are often highly politicized. It would, however, be a serious oversimplification to suppose that the only players on the field are traditional believers who insist on calling God "Father" and atheists who are trying to use religion as a political tool. Many people who regard the Bible as an authoritative text revealed by God also object to the exclusive use of male pronouns and images to refer to God. And in between the traditional believers and those whose approach to religion is a purely instrumental one, there are large numbers of half-believers, proponents of new religions, people who advocate a return to pagan religions, and a lot of people who are just generally bewildered about what to think. People are often in internal conflict about their religious beliefs, and determining when a person has abandoned enough of the traditional teachings of a religion to be classified as no longer adhering to it can be difficult. The purpose of this book is simply to get the important arguments for and against calling God "Father" out in the open. The essays collected here, then, include both critics of traditional religious language and responses by more traditional believers.

Reasons Given Against Calling God "Father"

Why have people objected to the use of paternal imagery to refer to God? In discussing this, we need to distinguish between reasons why a given individual might be uncomfortable with such imagery, and reasons that should persuade other people to either reject the religion entirely or insist that the religious community in question cease using masculine imagery to refer to God in its worship services. Painful experiences with one's father, for example, might make the use of the term *Father* to refer to God a stumbling block for some would-be believers. Most critics of traditional language about God, however, offer reasons for preferring other language that are not simply based on their own experiences or feelings, since others may have had quite different experiences that lead them to prefer traditional language. Bad relationships with one's father, although common, are not universal, and many people have had equally bad relationships with their mothers.

There are, broadly speaking, three different types of criticism that have been offered of the use of paternal imagery to talk about God. One objection, which emanates from the religious traditions themselves, is that exclusive use of paternal imagery leaves out important aspects of God's self-revelation in Scripture. (Richard Davis and Susanne Heine emphasize this point.) A second objection is that calling God "Father" reinforces a patriarchal social structure (a hierarchical one in which women are consistently kept in a subordinate position) and is therefore damaging to women. (Carol Christ, Elizabeth Johnson, and Rosemary Radford Ruether all make this type of argument.) And the third objection, made by ecologists, is that the emphasis on the transcendence of God conveyed by paternal imagery has led to an overemphasis on human superiority over the rest of nature (since human beings are said to be created "in the image of God"), and that this has encouraged human beings to adopt a manipulative and exploitative approach toward nature. Ecofeminists (represented in this collection by Rosemary Radford Ruether) combine the second and third objections, arguing that oppression of women and exploitation of nature are interconnected phenomena. Some serious believers concede that their religious tradition has, in fact, interpreted some passages of Scripture in ways that license oppression of women or exploitation of nature, but insist that such interpretations are one-sided and distorted and that, taken as a whole and rightly understood, the revealed scriptures do not license these sorts of sinful behavior. Tamar Frankiel and Edith Black take this approach, and Leila Ahmad (listed in the For Further Reading section) makes the same sort of argument for the *Koran*.

Preview of Readings

The first reading, by Mircea Eliade, documents the pervasive use of parental imagery in human religious history, particularly the pattern in which the sky god associated with the vast celestial vault is called "lord," "chief," "father," or "most high," while the Earth is regarded as sacred and conceived as the Cosmic Mother who gives birth to all things. The second reading is from the creation story in the Book of Genesis and provides the biblical background for the subsequent articles. There are two slightly different accounts of creation. Scholars generally take the second one (in Genesis 2) to have an earlier historical origin, since it is less abstract and theologically sophisticated and describes God as forming Adam from the dust of the ground and breathing into his nostrils the breath of life. Genesis 3 describes the fall of Adam and Eve and their expulsion from paradise.

God the Father and the Legitimation of Patriarchy

Carol Christ, in the selection here, rejects Judaism and Christianity because she believes that religions that think of the Supreme Being as male produce an association in people's minds between masculinity and the exercise of power, so that the exercise of power by women is regarded as anomalous or suspect in some way. God symbolism in Christianity undergirds the interests of men in patriarchy by creating certain sorts of moods and motivations. Worship of the Great Goddess is, she believes, necessary for the empowerment of women—to help them affirm the legitimacy and beneficence of female power. Worship of the Great Goddess will, she argues, help women to trust in their own power, celebrate their bodies, and believe that they can achieve their own wills in the world.

Elizabeth Johnson's position is more nuanced. She does not begin with a root-and-branch rejection of the Judeo-Christian tradition, as Carol Christ does. Starting instead from the theological point that God is, after all, wholly ineffable, and no human language can truly describe

God's being, she argues that to fix on masculine imagery is a kind of idolatry—putting the image of a created thing in place of God. Since no language is adequate to God, she therefore concludes that it is legitimate to bring in nontheological reasons for using feminine pronouns to refer to God—for example, its effect on the social and political position of women. She considers and rejects other ways of balancing exclusive use of male imagery by emphasizing the feminine aspects of God while still thinking of God predominantly as "Father," or by feminizing the Holy Spirit. Ultimately she hopes that people will be able to use male and female images equally to talk about God, but in order to correct for the longstanding androcentric bias in God-language and reorient our imaginations and recover the dignity of women created in the image of God, it is necessary now to deliberately employ feminine images to describe and name the divine.

Juli Loesch Wiley takes issue with those feminists who claim that thinking of God as "Father" supports patriarchy. She argues that, in fact, the authority of God the Father provides a check on the power of human fathers, since God stands in judgment of them and holds them accountable if they violate the God-given rights of women and children. She also notes that Christians call God "Father" because Jesus did (since God *was* his father) and that Christians, being "baptized into Christ," take on the same relationship to God that Jesus had. Finally, she argues that feminist psychoanalytic theory itself suggests that thinking of God as "Mother" could be disastrous. And, in her "In Defense of the Male Priesthood," Wiley argues that Jesus envisioned a servant priesthood, and that the vows of poverty, chastity, and obedience function as a kind of school of humility for men to curb male tendencies to be dominating, sexually aggressive, power hungry, and self-aggrandizing. Richard Davis, like Wiley, emphasizes the prophetic dimension of religion and sees God as a being with power, authority, and majesty, who stands in judgment of us and our ways. Since he does not regard God as merely a projection of the human psyche, Davis evaluates religious language in terms of the way it facilitates or impedes the worshipper's relationship with God. While noting that the Bible contains many passages in which feminine imagery is used to describe God, he opposes those who wish to feminize God by excluding male symbols, male images, and male pronouns from the common worship of the Christian community. The feminization of God is of more than merely theoretical interest to him because, as a gay man, he personally tends to think of God as a masculine lover.

Susanne Heine emphasizes the transcendence of God as a check on the uses of both masculine and feminine imagery. She argues that if those who are abused by their fathers can find consolation in the figure of a heavenly Mother, those with abusive mothers can find consolation in the figure of a heavenly Father. For that matter, those with abusive fathers could find in God the good Father they need and be healed of their emotional wounds in this way.

Gary Culpepper responds directly to Elizabeth Johnson. As a theologian, he devotes comprehensive attention to the complex patterns of naming persons, human and divine, in Scripture and Christian tradition, with particular attention directed to the practice of Jesus himself. At stake is the distinction between metaphorical and "more-than-metaphorical" speech in the practice of naming God. This distinction is important for Christian belief and life, as it is integral to the identification of the Persons of God in their distinction from one another, and in their common activity for the salvation of all human beings, male and female alike.

The Ecofeminist Critique

Ecofeminists (represented here by Rosemary Radford Ruether) argue that by employing masculine imagery in thinking of God, we set up an ontological hierarchy in which males are above females—that is, males more nearly reflect God's image as spiritual, rational, and transcendent, while females are identified with the body, emotion, and nature. Thus, not only do human beings generally see themselves as entitled to dominate and use nature in any way they want, since they have a mental or spiritual dimension the rest of creation lacks, but within the human species male human beings are higher than females on this same scale, and are thus entitled to dominate and use them.

The positive vision of the ecofeminists emphasizes our immanence in nature and the interconnectedness of human beings with each other and with nature. Hierarchical dualism, in which spirit is separated from nature and regarded as superior to it, should be abandoned in favor of a more holistic and organic vision of human beings as part of nature. Nonviolence and egalitarianism are also important in a way that they are not for people like Carol Christ. The ecofeminist critique of the status quo is thus a deeper one, since ecofeminists are not just trying to move women up the ladder into more powerful positions in society, but are also envisioning radical social changes that would make society more egalitarian. Edith Black responds to the ecofeminists by analyzing the first three chapters of Genesis, pointing out that Adam and Eve are equally in the image of God, and that there is nothing in the text to indicate that women are less rational or more carnal than men. Since the sin of both Adam and Eve was one of disobeying God by wanting to become like God oneself—living forever and having knowledge of good and evil—it would seem that Eve was more in the grip of inordinate spiritual ambition than carnal desire (she did not, after all, eat the fruit for its taste). The fact that Eve is held responsible for her action and punished clearly indicates that she is regarded by God as a rational being with free will just as much as Adam is. And, Black argues, the text of Genesis 3 indicates that patriarchy is a result of the Fall, and not part of God's original intention.

Finally, she argues, feminists have tended to focus too much on the sin of Eve, neglecting the essential role played by Mary, the mother of Jesus, in the salvation of humankind (she has been accorded the title "Mother of God" by the Church). Also called the "second Eve," Mary, by cooperating with God's plan, reversed the sin of disobedience committed by Adam and Eve and made reconciliation with God possible by giving birth to the Redeemer. As the greatest of the saints, she stands as a model of perfected humanity.

Tamar Frankiel responds to the ecofeminist argument from within the Jewish tradition, arguing that the sort of mind/body or spirit/matter dualism the ecofeminists criticize is Greek and not Hebraic in origin, and that God's transcendence should not be understood in terms of His being made of different (spiritual) stuff, but that His transcendence is exemplified most in His mercy because it comes from a place beyond the natural order of things. God breaks into history; His thoughts and ways are not our thoughts and ways. Therefore, human beings who are in the image of God should not be understood in dualistic terms in which the mind is distinct from and higher than the body; both men and women are embodied, and both possess equally what is distinctively human—namely: will, creativity, reason, and language.

Difference Feminism

Wolf-Devine, in her essay "Difference Feminism and the Role of Women in the Church," explores the thought of the difference feminists inspired by Carol Gilligan and connects their thought with the role of women in the church. In contrast to assimilationist feminism, which treats men and women as interchangeable "persons," difference feminism, rather than focusing on the priesthood exclusively, invites us to widen our focus and think about places where women's special talents are needed in the church.

Questions for Reflection

1. Is it possible to think of God as personal without employing concepts that involve gender?
2. To what extent do you think that religious belief of any kind is something you can simply choose?
3. Some people have argued that if religion is to perform a prophetic role, as it did for the Reverend Martin Luther King—in other words, if it is to place existing practices and institutions under judgment—it must respect God's transcendence (that is, His existing mysteriously outside both nature and society). Do you agree?

4. Lenin regarded religion as functioning to reflect and ratify existing power relationships, and many feminists have applied this to male-female relationships, claiming that religion functions as a prop for the patriarchal status quo. But if one accepts this sort of view of religion, does it make sense to try to use it for radical (or even moderate) social critique?
5. Patriarchy was originally a Roman system in which men had life-and-death power over their wives and children. The term is now used rather loosely. In what sense, if any, do you think the United States is now a patriarchy? Is it a matter of how many women are in political and economic leadership positions, or is patriarchy to be found in intimate male-female relationships? If the latter, does it seem to you, on the basis of your own experience, that men invariably dominate in marriages or other intimate relationships, or do women dominate sometimes also? Or do most couples divide which areas each controls in a balanced way?

The Sacredness of Nature and Cosmic Religion

Sky Gods and Mother Earth

MIRCEA ELIADE

Mircea Eliade points out that for the religious person, nature is never only "natural"—it is always fraught with a religious value. The gods manifested the different modalities of the sacred in the very structure of the cosmos. In this context, he discusses both the remote Sky God, and the Earth imagined as Mother.

For religious man, nature is never only "natural"; it is always fraught with a religious value. This is easy to understand, for the cosmos is a divine creation; coming from the hands of the gods, the world is impregnated with sacredness. It is not simply a sacrality *communicated* by the gods, as is the case, for example, with a place or an object consecrated by the divine presence. The gods did more; *they manifested the different modalities of the sacred in the very structure of the world and of cosmic phenomena.*

The world stands displayed in such a manner that, in contemplating it, religious man discovers the many modalities of the sacred, and hence of being. Above all, the world exists, it is there, and it has a structure; it is not a chaos but a cosmos, hence it presents itself as creation, as work of the gods. This divine work always preserves its quality of transparency, that is, it spontaneously reveals the many aspects of the sacred. The sky directly, "naturally," reveals the infinite distance, the transcendence of the deity. The earth too is transparent; it presents itself as universal mother and nurse. The cosmic rhythms manifest order, harmony, permanence, fecundity. The cosmos as a whole is an organism at once *real, living,* and *sacred;* it simultaneously reveals the modalities of being and of sacrality [sacredness]. Ontophany [manifestation of being] and hierophany [manifestation of the sacred] meet.

Excerpt from *The Sacred and the Profane: The Nature of Religion* by Mircea Eliade, by Rowohlt Taschenbuch Verlag GmbH, English translation 1959 and renewed 1987 by Harcourt, Inc. Reprinted by permission of the publisher.

In this chapter we shall try to understand how the world presents itself to the eyes of religious man—or, more precisely, how sacrality is revealed through the very structures of the world. We must not forget that for religious man the supernatural is indissolubly connected with the natural, that nature always expresses something that transcends it. As we said earlier: a sacred stone is venerated because it is *sacred,* not because it is a *stone;* it is the sacrality *manifested through the mode of being of the stone* that reveals its true essence. This is why we cannot speak of naturism [identification of nature with God] or of natural religion in the sense that the nineteenth century gave to those terms; for it is "supernature" that the religious man apprehends through the natural aspects of the world.

The Celestial Sacred and the Uranian Gods

Simple contemplation of the celestial vault already provokes a religious experience. The sky shows itself to be infinite, transcendent. It is pre-eminently the "wholly other" than the little represented by man and his environment. Transcendence is revealed by simple awareness of infinite height. "Most high" spontaneously becomes an attribute of divinity. The higher regions inaccessible to man, the sidereal [relating to stars or constellations] zones, acquire the momentousness of the transcendent, of absolute reality, of eternity. There dwell the gods; there a few privileged mortals make their way by rites of ascent; there, in the conception of certain religions, mount the souls of the dead. The "most high" is a dimension inaccessible to man as man; it belongs to superhuman forces and beings. He who ascends by mounting the steps of a sanctuary or the ritual ladder that leads to the sky ceases to be a man; in one way or another, he shares in the divine condition.

All this is not arrived at by a logical, rational operation. The transcendental category of height, of the super-terrestrial, of the infinite, is revealed to the whole man, to his intelligence and his soul. It is a total awareness on man's part; beholding the sky, he simultaneously discovers the divine incommensurability and his own situation in the cosmos. For the sky, *by its own mode of being,* reveals transcendence, force, eternity. It *exists absolutely* because it is *high, infinite, eternal, powerful.*

This is the true significance of the statement made above—that the gods manifested the different modalities of the sacred in the very structure of the world. In other words, the cosmos—paradigmatic work of the gods—is so constructed that a religious sense of the divine transcendence is aroused by the very existence of the sky. And since the sky *exists* absolutely, many of the supreme gods of primitive peoples are called by names designating height, the celestial vault, meteorological phenomena, or simply Owner of the Sky or Sky Dweller.

The supreme divinity of the Maori is named Iho; *iho* means elevated, high up. Uwoluwu, the supreme god of the Akposo Negroes, signifies what is on high, the upper regions. Among the Selk'nam of Tierra del Fuego God is called Dweller in the Sky or He Who Is in the Sky. Puluga, the supreme being of the Andaman Islanders, dwells in the sky; the thunder is his voice, wind his breath, the storm is the sign of his anger, for with his lightning he punishes those who break his commandments. The Sky God of the Yoruba of the Slave Coast is named Olorun, literally Owner of the Sky. The Samoyed worship Num, a god who dwells in the highest sky and whose name means sky. Among the Koryak, the supreme divinity is called the One on High, the Master of the High, He Who Exists. The Ainu know him as the Divine Chief of the Sky, the Sky God, the Divine Creator of the Worlds, but also as *Kamui*, that is, Sky. The list could easily be extended.

We may add that the same situation is found in the religions of more civilized peoples, that is, of peoples who have played an important role in history....

There is no question of naturism [identification of nature with God] here. The celestial god is not identified with the sky, for he is the same god who, creating the entire cosmos, created the sky too. This is why he is called Creator, All-Powerful, Lord, Chief, Father, and the like. The celestial god is a person, not a uranian [of the sky] epiphany [showing forth or manifestation]. But he lives in the sky and is manifested in meteorological phenomena—thunder, lightning, storms, meteors, and so on. This means that certain privileged structures of the cosmos—the sky, the atmosphere—constitute favorite epiphanies of the supreme being; he reveals his presence by what is specifically and peculiarly his—the majesty (*majestas*) of the celestial immensity, the terror (*tremendum*) of the storm.

The Remote God

The history of supreme beings whose structure is celestial is of the utmost importance for an understanding of the religious history of humanity as a whole. We cannot even consider writing that history here, in a few pages. But we must at least refer to a fact that to us seems primary. Celestially structured supreme beings tend to disappear from the practice of religion, from cult; they depart from among men, withdraw to the sky, and become remote, inactive gods (*dei otiose*). In short, it may be said of these gods that, after creating the cosmos, life, and man, they feel a sort of fatigue, as if the immense enterprise of the Creation had exhausted their resources. So they withdraw to the sky, leaving a son or a demiurge on earth to finish or perfect the Creation. Gradually their place is taken by other divine figures—the mythical ancestors, the mother-goddesses, the fecundating gods, and the like. The god of the storm still preserves a celestial structure, but he is no longer a creating supreme being; he is only the fecundator [one who makes fertile] of the earth, sometimes he is only a helper to his companion (*paredros*), the earth-mother. The celestially structured supreme being preserves his preponderant place only among pastoral peoples, and he attains a unique situation in religions that tend to monotheism (Ahura-Mazda) or that are fully monotheistic (Yahweh, Allah)....

The Dweller in the Sky or He Who Is in the Sky of the Selk'nam is eternal, omniscient, all-powerful, the creator; but the Creation was finished by the mythical ancestors, who had also been made by the supreme god before he withdrew to a place above the stars. For now this god has isolated himself from men, is indifferent to the affairs of the world. He has neither images nor priests. Prayers are addressed to him only in case of sickness. "Thou who art above, take not my child; he is still too young!" Offerings are rarely made to him except during storms.

It is the same among many African peoples; the great celestial god, the supreme being, all-powerful creator, plays only a minor role in the religious life of most tribes. He is too far away or too good to need an actual cult, and he is invoked only in extreme cases....

It is useless to multiply examples. Everywhere in these primitive religions the celestial supreme being appears to have lost *religious currency;* he has no place in the cult, and in the myths he draws farther and farther away from man until he becomes a *deus otiosus*. Yet he is remembered and entreated as the last resort, *when all ways of appealing to other gods and goddesses, the ancestors, and the demons, have failed.* As the Oraons express it: "Now we have tried everything, but we still have you to help us." And they sacrifice a white cock to him, crying, "God, thou art our creator, have mercy on us."

The Religious Experience of Life

The divine remoteness actually expresses man's increasing interest in his own religious, cultural, and economic discoveries. Through his concern with hierophanies of life, through discovering the sacral fertility....

It could be said that the very structure of the cosmos keeps memory of the celestial supreme being alive. It is as if the gods had created the world in such a way that it could not but reflect their existence; for no world is possible without verticality, and that dimension alone is enough to evoke transcendence.

Driven from religious life in the strict sense, the *celestial sacred* remains active through symbolism. A religious symbol conveys its message even if it is no longer *consciously* understood in every part. For a symbol speaks to the whole human being and not only to the intelligence....

Terra Mater

An Indian prophet, Smohalla, chief of the Wanapum tribe, refused to till the ground. He held that it was a sin to mutilate and tear up the earth, mother of all. He said: "You ask me to plow the ground! Shall I take a knife and tear my mother's bosom? Then when I die she will not take me to her bosom to rest. You ask me to dig for stone! Shall I dig under her skin for her bones? Then when I die, I cannot enter her body to be born again. You ask me to cut grass and make hay and sell it, and be rich like white men! But how dare I cut off my mother's hair?"

These words were spoken scarcely fifty years ago. But they come to us from very far. The emotion that we feel on hearing them arises primarily from their revealing to us, with incomparable freshness and spontaneity, the primordial image of Mother Earth. The image is found throughout the world in countless forms and variants. It is the *Terra Mater* or *Tellus Mater* so familiar to Mediterranean religions, who gives birth to all beings. "Concerning Earth, the mother of all, shall I sing," we read in the Homeric *Hymn to Earth,* "firm earth, eldest of gods, that nourishes all things in the world. . . . Thine it is to give or to take life from mortal men."

. . . And in the *Choephori* Aeschylus celebrates the earth "who bringeth all things to birth, reareth them, and receiveth again into her womb."

The prophet Smohalla does not tell us in what way men are born of the telluric [of the Earth] mother. But North American myths reveal how things happened in the beginning, *in illo tempore.* The first men lived for a certain time in the breast of their mother, that is, in the depths of the earth. There in the telluric abyss they led a half-human life; in some sort they were still imperfectly formed embryos. At least so said the Lenni-Lenape or Delaware Indians, who once inhabited Pennsylvania. According to their myths, although the Creator had already prepared on the surface of the earth all the things that men now enjoy there, he had decided that these first men should remain yet a while hidden in the bosom of the telluric mother, so that they might better develop, might ripen. Other American Indian myths speak of an ancient time when Mother Earth brought forth human beings in the same way that she now produces bushes and reeds. . . .

The dying man desires to return to Mother Earth, to be buried in his native soil. "Crawl to the Earth, thy mother," says the *Rig Veda* (X, 18, 10). "Thou who art earth, I put thee in the Earth!" . . .

Humi Positio: Laying the Infant on the Ground

. . . This fundamental experience—that the human mother is only the representative of the telluric Great Mother—has given rise to countless customs. We will mention, as an example, giving birth on the ground (*humi positio*), a ritual that is found almost all over the world, from Australia to China, from Africa to South America....

The religious meaning of the custom is easy to see: generation and childbirth are microcosmic versions of a paradigmatic act performed by the earth; every human mother only imitates and repeats this primordial act of the appearance of life in the womb of the earth. Hence every mother must put herself in contact with the Great Genetrix, that she may be guided by her in accomplishing the mystery that is the birth of a life, may receive her beneficent energies and secure her maternal protection.

Still more widely disseminated is the laying of the infant on the ground. In some parts of Europe it is still the custom today to lay the infant on the ground as soon as it has been bathed and swaddled. The father then takes the child up from the ground (*de terra tollere*) to show his gratitude. In ancient China "the dying man, like the newborn infant, is laid on the ground.... To be born or to die, to enter the living family or the ancestral family (and to leave the one or the other), there is a common threshold, one's native Earth.... When the newborn infant or the dying man is laid on the Earth, it is for her to say if the birth or the death are valid, if they are to be taken as accomplished and normal facts...."

Initiation includes a ritual death and resurrection. This is why, among numerous primitive peoples, the novice is symbolically "killed," laid in a trench, and covered with leaves. When he rises from the grave he is looked upon as a *new man,* for he has been brought to birth once more, this time *directly by the cosmic Mother.*

Woman, then, is mystically held to be one with the earth, childbearing is seen as a variant on the human scale, of the telluric fertility. All religious experiences connected with fecundity and birth *have a cosmic structure.* The sacrality of woman depends on the holiness of the earth. Feminine fecundity has a cosmic model—that of Terra Mater, the universal Genetrix.

In some religions Mother Earth is imagined as capable of conceiving alone, without the assistance of a coadjutor. Traces of such archaic ideas are still found in the myths of the parthenogenesis of Mediterranean goddesses. According to Hesiod, Gaia (= Earth) gave birth to Ouranos "a being equal to herself, able to cover her completely" (*Theogony,* 126 ff). Other Greek goddesses likewise gave birth without the help of gods. This is a mythical expression of the self-sufficiency and fecundity of Mother Earth. Such mythical conceptions have their counterparts in beliefs concerning the spontaneous fecundity of woman and in her occult magico-religious powers, which exert a determining influence on plant life. The social and cultural phenomenon known as matriarchy is connected with the discovery of agriculture by woman. It was woman who first cultivated food plants. Hence it is she who becomes owner of the soil and crops. The magico-religious prestige and consequent social predominance of woman have a cosmic model—the figure of Mother Earth.

THE SACREDNESS OF NATURE AND COSMIC RELIGION

In other religions the cosmic creation, or at least its completion, is the result of a hierogamy [sacred marriage] between the Sky-God and Mother Earth. This cosmogonic myth [having to do with the origin of the world] is quite widely disseminated. It is found especially in Oceania—from Indonesia to Micronesia—but it also occurs in Asia, Africa, and the two Americas. Now, as we have seen, the cosmogonic myth is pre-eminently the paradigmatic myth; it serves as a model for human behavior. This is why human marriage is regarded as an imitation of the cosmic hierogamy. "I am Heaven," the husband proclaims in the *Brihadarnyaka Upanishad* (VI, 4, 20), "thou art Earth!" Even so early as the *Atharva Veda* (XIV, 2, 71) groom and bride are assimilated to heaven and earth. Dido celebrates her marriage to Aeneas in the midst of a violent storm (*Aeneid,* IV, 165 ff); their union coincides with that of the elements; the Sky embraces his wife, dispensing the fertilizing rain. In Greece marriage rites imitated the example of Zeus's secret union with Hera (Pausanias, II, 36, 2). As we should expect, the divine myth is the paradigmatic model for the human union. But there is another aspect which requires emphasis—*the cosmic structure of the conjugal ritual,* and hence of human sexual behavior. For nonreligious man of the modern societies, this simultaneously *cosmic* and *sacred* dimension of conjugal union is difficult to grasp. But as we have had occasion to say more than once, it must not be forgotten that religious man of the archaic societies sees the world as fraught with messages. Sometimes the messages are in cipher [code], but the myths are there to help man decipher them. As we shall see later, the whole of human experience can be homologized to [made to have the same structure as] cosmic life, hence can be sanctified, for the cosmos is the supreme creation of the gods.

Ritual orgies for the benefit of crops likewise have a divine model—the hierogamy of the Fecundating God and Mother Earth. The fertility of the fields is stimulated by an unlimited genetic frenzy. From one point of view the orgy corresponds to the pre-Creation state of non-differentiation. This is why certain New Year ceremonies include orgiastic rites: social confusion, sexual license, and saturnalia symbolize regression to the amorphous condition that preceded the Creation of the World. In the case of a creation on the level of vegetable life, this cosmologico-ritual scenario is repeated, for the new crop is equivalent to a new creation. The idea of *renewal*—which we encountered in New Year rituals whose purpose was at once the renewal of time and the regeneration of the world—recurs in orgiastic agricultural scenarios. Here too the orgy is a return to the cosmic night, the preformal, the waters, in order to ensure complete regeneration of life and hence the fertility of the earth and an abundance of crops.

Questions for Reflection on Mircea Eliade

1. Explain what Eliade means in saying "For religious man, nature is never only 'natural.'"
2. How do Sky Gods differ from divinities connected with fertility and the Earth? Sky Gods are almost universally thought of as male and Earth Goddesses as female. Why? Does this make sense to you? Try to think of the earth as father and the sky as mother. Does it work just as well? Why or why not?
3. Supposing we think of the earth as mother and the sky as father, does the fact that the sky is spatially above the earth imply that the Sky God is more powerful, or are there reasons why Mother Earth might be thought of as more powerful?
4. The sacredness of the Earth in cosmic religion is a function of her power to give birth to all living things (sometimes alone and sometimes as a result of her sacred union with the Sky God). In either case, motherhood and fertility are viewed very positively. It would seem, therefore, that those who seek to return to the tradition of worshipping the Earth as a Goddess ought to hold motherhood in particularly high esteem and value fertility. But this does not seem to be true of most of the ecologists, feminists, and ecofeminists who advocate return to such religions. Are they being inconsistent?

Genesis

Chapters 1–3

The Book of Genesis describes the creation of the world and humanity, followed by the Fall, as traditionally understood within the Jewish and Christian traditions. In order to avoided biasing issues, we have used the Revised Standard Version of the Bible, *which was prepared and won widespread acceptance among Christians of all theological persuasions before the current round of controversy about sex and gender issues within the churches.*

In the beginning God created the heavens and the earth. ²The earth was without form and void, and darkness was upon the face of the deep; and the Spirit of God was moving over the face of the waters.

³And God said, "Let there be light"; and there was light. ⁴And God saw that the light was good; and God separated the light from the darkness. ⁵God called the light Day, and the darkness he called Night. And there was evening and there was morning, one day.

⁶And God said, "Let there be a firmament in the midst of the waters, and let it separate the waters from the waters." ⁷And God made the firmament and separated the waters which were under the firmament from the waters which were above the firmament. And it was so. ⁸And God called the firmament Heaven. And there was evening and there was morning, a second day.

⁹And God said, "Let the waters under the heavens be gathered together into one place, and let the dry land appear." And it was so. ¹⁰God called the dry land Earth, and the waters that were gathered together he called Seas. And God saw that it was good. ¹¹And God said, "Let the earth

Genesis 1–3 From Revised Standard Version of the Bible, 1971 by Division of Christian Education of the National Council of Churches of Christ in the USA, used by permission.

put forth vegetation, plants yielding seed, and fruit trees bearing fruit in which is their seed, each according to its kind, upon the earth." And it was so. [12]The earth brought forth vegetation, plants yielding seed according to their own kinds, and trees bearing fruit in which is their seed, each according to its kind. And God saw that it was good. [13]And there was evening and there was morning, a third day.

[14]And God said, "Let there be lights in the firmament of the heavens to separate the day from the night and let them be for signs and for seasons and for days and years, [15]and let them be lights in the firmament of the heavens to give light upon the earth." And it was so. [16]And God made the two great lights, the greater light to rule the day and the lesser light to rule the night; he made the stars also. [17]And God set them in the firmament of the heavens to give light upon the earth, [18]to rule over the day and over the night, and to separate the light from the darkness. And God saw that it was good. [19]And there was evening and there was morning, a fourth day.

[20]And God said, "Let the waters bring forth swarms of living creatures, and let birds fly above the earth across the firmament of the heavens." [21]So God created the great sea monsters and every living creature that moves, with which the waters swarm, according to their kinds, and every winged bird according to its kind. And God saw that it was good. [22]And God blessed them, saying, "Be fruitful and multiply and fill the waters in the seas, and let birds multiply on the earth." [23]And there was evening and there was morning, a fifth day.

[24]And God said, "Let the earth bring forth living creatures according to their kinds: cattle and creeping things and beasts of the earth according to their kinds." And it was so. [25]And God made the beasts of the earth according to their kinds and the cattle according to their kinds, and everything that creeps upon the ground according to its kind. And God saw that it was good.

[26]Then God said, "Let us make man in our image, after our likeness; and let them have dominion over the fish of the sea, and over the birds of the air, and over the cattle, and over all the earth, and over every creeping thing that creeps upon the earth." [27]So God created man in his own image, in the image of God he created him; male and female he created them. [28]And God blessed them, and God said to them, "Be fruitful and multiply, and fill the earth and subdue it; and have dominion over the fish of the sea and over the birds of the air and over every living thing that moves upon the earth." [29]And God said, "Behold, I have given you every plant yielding seed which is upon the face of all the earth, and every tree with seed in its fruit you shall have them for food. [30]And to every beast of the earth, and to every bird of the air, and to everything that creeps on the earth, everything that has the breath of life, I have given every green plant for food." And it was so. [31]And God saw everything that he had made, and behold, it was very good. And there was evening and there was morning, a sixth day.

2 Thus the heavens and the earth were finished, and all the host of them. ²And on the seventh day God finished his work which he had done, and he rested on the seventh day from all his work which he had done. ³So God blessed the seventh day and hallowed it, because on it God rested from all his work which he had done in creation.

⁴These are the generations of the heavens and the earth when they were created.

In the day that the Lord God made the earth and the heavens, ⁵when no plant of the field was yet in the earth and no herb of the field had yet sprung up—for the Lord God had not caused it to rain upon the earth, and there was no man to till the ground; ⁶but a mist went up from the earth and watered the whole face of the ground—⁷then the Lord God formed man of dust from the ground, and breathed into his nostrils the breath of life; and man became a living being. ⁸And the Lord God planted a garden in Eden, in the east; and there he put the man whom he had formed.

⁹And out of the ground the Lord God made to grow every tree that is pleasant to the sight and good for food, the tree of life also in the midst of the garden, and the tree of the knowledge of good and evil.

¹⁰A river flowed out of Eden to water the garden, and there it divided and became four rivers. ¹¹The name of the first is Pishon; it is the one which flows around the whole land of Hav'ilah, where there is gold; ¹²and the gold of that land is good; bdellium and onyx stone are there. ¹³The name of the second river is Gihon; it is the one which flows around the whole land of Cush. ¹⁴And the name of the third river is Hid'dekel, which flows east of Assyria. And the fourth river is the Euphra'tes.

¹⁵The Lord God took the man and put him in the garden of Eden to till it and keep it. ¹⁶And the Lord God commanded the man, saying, "You may freely eat of every tree of the garden; ¹⁷but of the tree of the knowledge of good and evil you shall not eat, for in the day that you eat of it you shall die."

¹⁸Then the Lord God said, "It is not good that the man should be alone; I will make him a helper fit for him." ¹⁹So out of the ground the Lord God formed every beast of the field and every bird of the air, and brought them to the man to see what he would call them; and whatever the man called every living creature, that was its name. ²⁰The man gave names to all cattle, and to the birds of the air, and to every beast of the field; but for the man there was not found a helper fit for him. ²¹So the Lord God caused a deep sleep to fall upon the man, and while he slept took one of his ribs and closed up its place with flesh; ²²and the rib which the Lord God had taken from the man he made into a woman and brought her to the man. ²³Then the man said,

"This at last is bone of my bones and flesh of my flesh; she shall be called Woman, because she was taken out of Man."

²⁴"Therefore a man leaves his father and his mother and cleaves to his wife, and they become one flesh. ²⁵And the man and his wife were both naked, and were not ashamed.

3 Now the serpent was more subtle than any other wild creature that the Lord God had made. He said to the woman, "Did God say, 'You shall not eat of any tree of the garden'?" ²And the woman said to the serpent, "We may eat of the fruit of the trees of the garden; ³but God said, 'You shall not eat of the fruit of the tree which is in the midst of the garden, neither shall you touch it, lest you die.'"

⁴But the serpent said to the woman, "You will not die. ⁵For God knows that when you eat of it your eyes will be opened, and you will be like God, knowing good and evil." ⁶So when the woman saw that the tree was good for food, and that it was a delight to the eyes, and that the tree was to be desired to make one wise, she took of its fruit and ate; and she also gave some to her husband, and he ate. ⁷Then the eyes of both were opened, and they knew that they were naked; and they sewed fig leaves together and made themselves aprons.

⁸And they heard the sound of the Lord God walking in the garden in the cool of the day, and the man and his wife hid themselves from the presence of the Lord God among the trees of the garden. ⁹But the Lord God called to the man, and said to him, "Where are you?" ¹⁰And he said, "I heard the sound of thee in the garden, and I was afraid, because I was naked; and I hid myself." ¹¹He said, "Who told you that you were naked? Have you eaten of the tree of which I commanded you not to eat?" ¹²The man said, "The woman whom thou gavest to be with me, she gave me fruit of the tree, and I ate." ¹³Then the Lord God said to the woman, "What is this that you have done?" The woman said, "The serpent beguiled me, and I ate."

¹⁴The Lord God said to the serpent,
"Because you have done this,
cursed are you above all cattle,
and above all wild animals;
upon your belly you shall go,
and dust you shall eat
all the days of your life.
¹⁵I will put enmity between you and the woman,
and between your seed and her seed;
he shall bruise your head,
and you shall bruise his heel."
¹⁶To the woman he said,
"I will greatly multiply your pain in childbearing;

in pain you shall bring forth children,
yet your desire shall be for your husband,
and he shall rule over you."
[17]And to Adam he said,
"Because you have listened to the voice of
your wife,
and have eaten of the tree
of which I commanded you,
'You shall not eat of it,'
cursed is the ground because of you;
in toil you shall eat of it all the days of
your life;
[18]thorns and thistles it shall bring forth
to you;
and you shall eat the plants of the
field.
[19]In the sweat of your face
you shall eat bread
till you return to the ground,
for out of it you were taken;
you are dust,
and to dust you shall return."

[20]The man called his wife's name Eve, because she was the mother of all living. [21]And the LORD God made for Adam and for his wife garments of skins, and clothed them.

[22]Then the LORD God said, "Behold, the man has become like one of us, knowing good and evil; and now, lest he put forth his hand and take also of the tree of life, and eat, and live for ever"—[23]therefore the LORD God sent him forth from the garden of Eden, to till the ground from which he was taken. [24]He drove out the man; and at the east of the garden of Eden he placed the cherubim, and a flaming sword which turned every way, to guard the way to the tree of life.

Questions for Reflection on Genesis, Chapters 1–3

1. What is meant by saying human beings are in the image of God? What sort of things is God shown doing? Are these things people can also do? Are men and women both in the image of God? If so, does this mean that there is both male and female in God?

2. Do you think that Eve is portrayed as more to blame than Adam for taking the forbidden fruit? Does her taking the fruit first have any significance? Does God appear to hold them equally responsible?
3. Look closely at the differences between the way God creates human beings and the way he creates the world and the animals. What do these imply about how humans differ from animals? Also, how is Adam's relationship to Eve different from his relationship to the animals?
4. Does the text sanction patriarchy (male domination of females)?

Why Women Need the Goddess

Phenomenological, Psychological, and Political Reflections

CAROL P. CHRIST

Carol P. Christ discusses the phenomenological, psychological, and political ramifications of the emergence of the symbol of the Goddess among women. She maintains that this symbol has much to offer women who are struggling to get rid of powerful and pervasive devaluations of female power, and to create a new culture that celebrates women's power, bodies, and will.

At the close of Ntosake Shange's stupendously successful Broadway play *For Colored Girls Who Have Considered Suicide When the Rainbow Is Enuf*, a tall beautiful black woman rises from despair to cry out, "I found God in myself and I loved her fiercely." Her discovery is echoed by women around the country who meet spontaneously in small groups on full moons, solstices, and equinoxes to celebrate the Goddess as symbol of life and death powers and waxing and waning energies in the universe and in themselves.

It is the night of the full moon. Nine women stand in a circle, on a rocky hill above the city. The western sky is rosy with the setting sun; in the east the moon's face begins to peer above the horizon. . . . The woman pours out a cup of wine onto the earth, refills it, and raises it high. "Hail, Tana, Mother of mothers!" she cries. "Awaken from your long sleep, and return to your children again!"

What are the political and psychological effects of this fierce new love of the divine in themselves for women whose spiritual experience has been focused by the male God of Judaism and Christianity? Is the spiritual dimension of feminism a passing diversion, an escape from difficult but necessary political work? Or does the emergence of the symbol of Goddess among women have significant political and psychological ramifications for the feminist movement?

Reprinted with author permission. http://www.iupui.edu/~womrel/Rel433%20Readings/Christ_WhyWomenNeedGoddess.pdf

Religious symbol systems focused around exclusively male images of divinity create the impression that female power can never be fully legitimate or wholly beneficent. This message need never be explicitly stated (as, for example, it is in the story of Eve) for its effect to be felt. A woman completely ignorant of the myths of female evil in biblical religion nonetheless acknowledges the anomaly of female power when she prays exclusively to a male God. She may see herself as like God (created in the image of God) only by denying her own sexual identity and affirming God's transcendence of sexual identity. But she can never have the experience that is freely available to every man and boy in her culture, of having her full sexual identity affirmed as being in the image and likeness of God. In Geertz's terms, her "mood" is one of trust in male power as salvific and distrust of female power in herself and other women as inferior or dangerous. Such a powerful, pervasive, and long-lasting "mood" cannot fail to become a "motivation" that translates into social and political reality.

In *Beyond God the Father,* feminist theologian Mary Daly detailed the psychological and political ramifications of father religion for women. "If God in 'his' heaven is a father ruling his people," she wrote, "then it is the 'nature' of things and according to divine plan and the order of the universe that society be male dominated. Within this context, a *mystification of roles* takes place: The husband dominating his wife represents God 'himself.' The images and values of a given society have been projected into the realm of dogmas and 'Articles of Faith,' and these in turn justify the social structures which have given rise to them and which sustain their plausibility."

Philosopher Simone de Beauvoir was well aware of the function of patriarchal religion as legitimater of male power. As she wrote, "Man enjoys the great advantage of having a god endorse the code he writes; and since man exercises a sovereign authority over women it is especially fortunate that this authority has been vested in him by the Supreme Being. For the Jew, Mohammedans, and Christians, among others, man is Master by divine right; the fear of God will therefore repress any impulse to revolt in the downtrodden female."

This brief discussion of the psychological and political effects of God religion puts us in an excellent position to begin to understand the significance of the symbol of Goddess for women. In discussing the meaning of the Goddess, my method will first be phenomenological. I will isolate a meaning of the symbol of the Goddess as it has emerged in the lives of contemporary women. I will then discuss its psychological and political significance by contrasting the "moods" and "motivations" engendered by Goddess symbols with those engendered by Christian symbolism. I will also correlate Goddess symbolism with themes that have emerged in the women's movement, in order to show how Goddess symbolism undergirds and legitimates the concerns of the women's movement, much as God symbolism in Christianity undergirded the interests of men in patriarchy. I will discuss four aspects of Goddess symbolism here: the Goddess as affirmation of female power, the female body, the female will, and women's bonds and heritage. There are, of course, many other meanings of the Goddess that I will not discuss here.

The sources for the symbol of the Goddess in contemporary spirituality are traditions of Goddess worship and modern women's experience. The ancient Mediterranean, pre-Christian European, native American, Mesoamerican, Hindu, African, and other traditions are rich sources for Goddess symbolism. But these traditions are filtered through modern women's experiences. Traditions of Goddesses, subordinate to Gods, for example, are ignored. Ancient traditions are tapped selectively and eclectically, but they are not considered authoritative for modern consciousness. The Goddess symbol has emerged spontaneously in the dreams, fantasies, and thoughts of many women around the country in the past several years. . . .

The simplest and most basic meaning of the symbol of Goddess is the acknowledgment of the legitimacy of female power as a beneficent and independent power. A woman who echoes Ntosake Shange's dramatic statement, "I found God in myself and I loved her fiercely," is saying, "Female power is strong and creative." She is saying that the divine principle, the saving and sustaining power, is in herself, that she will no longer look to men or male figures as saviors. The strength and independence of female power can be intuited by contemplating ancient and modern images of the Goddess. This meaning of the symbol of Goddess is simple and obvious, and yet it is difficult for many to comprehend. It stands in sharp contrast to the paradigms of female dependence on males that have been predominant in Western religion and culture. . . .

. . . The affirmation of female power contained in the Goddess symbol has both psychological and political consequences. Psychologically, it means the defeat of the view engendered by patriarchy that women's power is inferior and dangerous. This new "mood" of affirmation of female power also leads to new "motivations"; it supports and undergirds women's trust in their own power and the power of other women in family and society.

If the simplest meaning of the Goddess symbol is an affirmation of the legitimacy and beneficence of female power, then a question immediately arises: "Is the Goddess simply female power writ large, and if so, why bother with the symbol of Goddess at all? Or does the symbol refer to a Goddess 'out there' who is not reducible to a human potential?" The many women who have rediscovered the power of Goddess would give three answers to this question: (1) The Goddess is divine female, a personification who can be invoked in prayer and ritual; (2) the Goddess is symbol of the life, death, and rebirth energy in nature and culture, in personal and communal life; and (3) the Goddess is symbol of the affirmation of the legitimacy and beauty of female power (made possible by the new becoming of women in the women's liberation movement. . . . Some would assert that the Goddess definitely is *not* "out there," that the symbol of a divinity "out there" is part of the legacy of patriarchal oppression, which brings with it the authoritarianism, hierarchicalism, and dogmatic rigidity associated with biblical monotheistic religions. . . . Others seem quite comfortable with the notion of Goddess as a divine female protector and creator and would find their experience of Goddess limited by the assertion that she is not *also* out there as well as within themselves and in all natural processes. When asked what the symbol of Goddess means, feminist priestess Starhawk replied, "It all depends on how I feel. When I feel weak, she is someone who can help and protect me. When I feel strong, she is the symbol of my own power. At other times I feel her as the natural energy in my body and the world." How are we to evaluate such a statement? Theologians might call these the words of a sloppy thinker. But my deepest intuition tells me they contain a wisdom that Western theological thought has lost. . . .

A second important implication of the Goddess symbol for women is the affirmation of the female body and the life cycle expressed in it. Because of women's unique position as menstruants, birthgivers, and those who have traditionally cared for the young and the dying, women's connection to the body, nature, and this world has been obvious. Women were denigrated because they seemed more carnal, fleshy, and earthy than the culture-creating males. The misogynist anti*body* tradition in Western thought is symbolized in the myth of Eve who is traditionally viewed as a sexual temptress, the epitome of women's carnal nature. This tradition reaches its nadir in the *Malleus Maleficarum (The Hammer of Evil-Doing Women),* which states, "All witchcraft stems from carnal lust, which in women is insatiable." The Virgin Mary, the positive female image in Christianity, does not contradict Christian denigration of the female body and its powers. The Virgin Mary is revered because she, in her perpetual virginity, transcends the carnal sexuality attributed to most women.

The denigration of the female body is expressed in cultural and religious taboos surrounding menstruation, childbirth, and menopause in women. While menstruation taboos may have originated in a perception of the awesome powers of the female body, they degenerated into a simple perception that there is something "wrong" with female bodily functions. Menstruating women were forbidden to enter the sanctuary in ancient Hebrew and premodern Christian communities. Although only Orthodox Jews still enforce religious taboos against menstruant women, few women in our culture grow up affirming their menstruation as a connection to sacred power. Most women learn that menstruation is a curse and grow up believing that the bloody facts of menstruation are best hidden away. Feminists challenge this attitude to the female body. . . .

The symbol of Goddess aids the process of naming and reclaiming the female body and its cycles and processes. In the ancient world and among modern women, the Goddess symbol represents the birth, death, and rebirth processes of the natural and human worlds. The female body is viewed as the direct incarnation of waxing and waning, life and death, cycles in the universe. This is sometimes expressed through the symbolic connection between the twenty-eight-day cycles of menstruation and the twenty-eight-day cycles of the moon. Moreover, the Goddess is celebrated in the triple aspect of youth, maturity, and age, or maiden, mother, and crone. The potentiality of the young girl is celebrated in the nymph or maiden aspect of the Goddess. The Goddess as mother is sometimes depicted giving birth, and giving birth is viewed as a symbol for all the creative, life-giving powers of the universe. The life-giving powers of the Goddess in her creative aspect are not limited to physical birth, for the Goddess is also seen as the creator of all the arts of civilization, including healing, writing, and the giving of just law. Women in the middle of life who are not physical mothers may give birth to poems, songs, and books, or nurture other women, men, and children. . . .

At the end of life, women incarnate the crone aspect of the Goddess. The wise old woman, the woman who knows from experience what life is about, the woman whose closeness to her own death gives her a distance and perspective on the problems of life, is celebrated as the third aspect of the Goddess. . . .

The possibilities of reclaiming the female body and its cycles have been expressed in a number of Goddess-centered rituals. Hallie Mountainwing and Barby My Own created a summer solstice ritual to celebrate menstruation and birth. The women simulated a birth canal and birthed each other into their circle. They raised power by placing their hands on each other's bellies and chanting together. Finally they marked each other's faces with rich, dark menstrual blood, saying, "This is the blood that promises renewal. This is the blood that promises sustenance. This is the blood that promises life." From hidden dirty secret to symbol of the life power of the Goddess, women's blood has come full circle. . . .

The "mood" created by the symbol of the Goddess in triple aspect is one of positive, joyful affirmation of the female body and its cycles and acceptance of aging and death as well as life. The "motivations" are to overcome menstrual taboos, to return the birth process to the hands of women, and to change cultural attitudes about age and death. Changing cultural attitudes toward the female body could go a long way toward overcoming the spirit-flesh, mind-body dualisms of Western culture, since, as Ruether has pointed out, the denigration of the female body is at the heart of these dualisms. The Goddess as symbol of the revaluation of the body and nature thus also undergirds the human potential and ecology movements. The "mood" is one of affirmation, awe, and respect for the body and nature, and the "motivation" is to respect the teachings of the body and the rights of all living beings.

A third important implication of the Goddess symbol for women is the positive valuation of will in a Goddess-centered ritual, especially in Goddess-centered ritual magic and spellcasting in womanspirit and feminist witchcraft circles. The basic notion behind ritual magic and spellcasting is energy as power. Here the Goddess is a center or focus of power and energy; she is the personification of the energy that flows between beings in the natural and human worlds. In Goddess circles, energy is raised by chanting or dancing. According to Starhawk, "Witches conceive of psychic energy as having form and substance that can be perceived and directed by those with a trained awareness. The power generated within the circle is built into a cone form, and at its peak is released—to the Goddess, to reenergize the members of the coven, or to do a specific work such as healing." In ritual magic, the energy raised is directed by willpower. Women who celebrate in Goddess circles believe they can achieve their wills in the world.

The emphasis on the will is important for women, because women traditionally have been taught to devalue their wills, to believe that they cannot achieve their will through their own power, and even to suspect that the assertion of will is evil. . . .

. . . Patriarchal religion has enforced the view that female initiative and will are evil through the juxtaposition of Eve and Mary. Eve caused the fall by asserting her will against the command of God, while Mary began the new age with her response to God's initiative, "Let it be done to me according to thy word" (Luke 1:38). Even for men, patriarchal religion values the passive will subordinate to divine initiative. The classical doctrines of sin and grace view sin as the prideful assertion of will and grace as the obedient subordination of the human will to the divine initiative or order. . . .

In a Goddess-centered context, in contrast, the will is valued. *A woman is encouraged to know her will, to believe that her will is valid, and to believe that her will can be achieved in the world,* three powers traditionally denied to her in patriarchy. In a Goddess-centered framework, a woman's will is not subordinated to the Lord God as king and ruler, nor to men as his representatives. Thus a woman is not reduced to waiting and acquiescing in the wills of others as she is in patriarchy. But neither does she adopt the egocentric form of will that pursues self-interest without regard for the interests of others.

The Goddess-centered context provides a different understanding of the will than that available in the traditional patriarchal religious framework. In the Goddess framework, will can be achieved only when it is exercised in harmony with the energies and wills of other beings. Wise women, for example, raise a cone of healing energy at the full moon or solstice when the lunar or solar energies are at their high points with respect to the earth. This discipline encourages them to recognize that not all times are propitious for the achieving of every will. Similarly, they know that spring is a time for new beginnings in work and love, summer a time for producing external manifestations of inner potentialities, and fall or winter times for stripping down to the inner core and extending roots. Such awareness of waxing and waning processes in the universe discourages arbitrary ego-centered assertion of will, while at the same time encouraging the assertion of individual will in cooperation with natural energies and the energies created by the wills of others. Wise women also have a tradition that whatever is sent out will be returned, and this reminds them to assert their wills in cooperative and healing rather than egocentric and destructive ways. This view of will allows women to begin to recognize, claim, and assert their wills without adopting the worst characteristics of the patriarchal understanding and use of will. In the Goddess-centered framework, the "mood" is one of positive affirmation of personal will in the context of the energies of other wills or beings. The "motivation" is for women to know and assert their wills in cooperation with other wills and energies. This of course does not mean that women always assert their wills in positive and life-affirming ways. Women's capacity for evil is, of course, as great as men's. My purpose is simply to contrast the differing attitudes toward the exercise of will *per se,* and the female will in particular, in Goddess-centered religion and in the Christian God-centered religion.

The fourth and final aspect of Goddess symbolism that I will discuss here is the significance of the Goddess for a revaluation of woman's bonds and heritage. . . . I will focus on the mother-daughter bond, in part because I believe it may be the key to the others.

Adrienne Rich has pointed out that the mother-daughter bond, perhaps the most important of woman's bonds, "resonant with charges . . . the flow of energy between two biologically alike bodies, one of which has lain in amniotic bliss inside the other, one of which has labored to give birth to the other," is rarely celebrated in patriarchal religion and culture. Christianity celebrates the father's relation to the son and the mother's relation to the son, but the story of mother and daughter is missing. So, too, in patriarchal literature and psychology the mothers and the daughters rarely exist. Volumes have been written about the Oedipal complex, but little has been written about the girl's relation to her mother. Moreover, as de Beauvoir has noted, the mother-daughter relation is distorted in patriarchy because the mother must give her daughter over to men in a male-defined culture in which women are viewed as inferior. The mother must socialize her daughter to become subordinate to men, and if her daughter challenges patriarchal norms, the mother is likely to defend the patriarchal structures against her own daughter. . . .

Almost the only story of mothers and daughters that has been transmitted in Western culture is the myth of Demeter and Persephone that was the basis of religious rites celebrated by women only, the Thesmophoria, and later formed the basis of the Eleusian mysteries, which were open to all who spoke Greek. In this story, the daughter, Persephone, is raped away from her mother, Demeter, by the God of the underworld. Unwilling to accept this state of affairs, Demeter rages and withholds fertility from the earth until her daughter is returned to her. What is important for women in this story is that a mother fights for her daughter and for her relation to her daughter. This is completely different from the mother's relation to her daughter in patriarchy. The "mood" created by the story of Demeter and Persephone is one of celebration of the mother-daughter bond, and the "motivation" is for mothers and daughters to affirm the heritage passed on from mother to daughter and to reject the patriarchal pattern where the primary loyalties of mother and daughter must be to men.

The symbol of Goddess has much to offer women who are struggling to be rid of the "powerful, pervasive, and long-lasting moods and motivations" of devaluation of female power, denigration of the female body, distrust of female will, and denial of the women's bonds and heritage that have been engendered by patriarchal religion. As women struggle to create a new culture in which women's power, bodies, will, and bonds are celebrated, it seems natural that the Goddess would reemerge as symbol of the newfound beauty, strength, and power of women.

Questions for Reflection on Carol P. Christ

1. What "moods" and "motivations" does Christ think are created by religions that center on worship of a male God? How does she think such religions support patriarchy? How might she answer Wiley on this point?
2. Christ sees Goddess symbolism as undergirding and legitimating the concerns of the women's movement (affirming female power, the female body, female will, and women's bonds and heritage) just as God symbolism in Christianity undergirded the interests of men in patriarchy. In order to arrive at an image of the Goddess, modern women have had to tap ancient religions selectively, omitting, for example, goddesses subordinate to gods. Is this just a case of subordinating religion to political goals (of the sort criticized by Davis)?
3. Suppose that you are persuaded by Carol Christ that goddess worship is necessary to liberate women and restore to them the dignity taken from them by patriarchy. A quick glance at history indicates that there have been a large number of different types of goddesses, embodying different images of female power. For example, there is Hera, the goddess of hearth and home, who got what she wanted out of Zeus by devious methods, and Aphrodite, goddess of unregulated sex (though not of a sort that seriously challenges male dominance). Demeter is the goddess of the Earth and of fertility. Kali represents the terrifying and destructive side to the mother goddess—the devouring mother, bringer of dissolution and death. How should you decide which one of them to worship? Would Christ encourage women to worship Kali, the Hindu Goddess of death? Why or why not? (See the section on Kali in the book by Harman listed in the For Further Reading section of this volume for more information.)
4. Can a person believe something because he or she believes it would be useful psychologically or politically to do so? Do you think Christ really believes in the Goddess?

5. Could a new religion founded by people who openly regarded it as a psychologically and politically useful fantasy make any converts (or is putting us in touch with a reality outside ourselves part of what it is to be a religion)? How might those who regard their religion as a deliberate projection of their group's ideals respond if they encountered another group—say conservative Muslims—who had different ideals and made strong truth claims for their religion?
6. Have actual goddess-worshipping societies in history had better track records when it comes to treating women with respect? If it turns out that they haven't, would this count against those who favor goddess worship as a way of improving women's social standing and self-esteem?
7. Although Roman Catholics and Eastern Orthodox Christians do not regard Mary as a goddess, she plays many of the same roles in their religious life that goddesses do: she offers believers an image of female perfection; she is regarded as holy and able through her prayers to help us in the troubles and sorrows of life; and she is a sympathetic mother, often contrasted with the harsh justice associated with God the Father and sometimes even with Jesus. Nonetheless, feminist theologians, and even more so feminist critics of Christianity, tend to be hostile or indifferent to Mary. Why do you think this is so?

Basic Linguistic Options

God, Women, Equivalence...

ELIZABETH JOHNSON

The holy mystery of God, Elizabeth Johnson maintains, is beyond all imagining. In the context of this avowal, she draws on women's interpreted experience, and critical retrieval of tradition, in order to develop a liberated way of naming God. This means speaking in female symbols for the divine mystery, testing their capacity to bear divine presence and power. Hopefully in the future we will be able to use both male and female images and symbols equally, but employing the female ones now is necessary to counterbalance the long-standing tradition of using male ones.

Why the Word "God"?

A certain liability attends the very word God, given the history of its use in androcentric theology. Insofar as it almost invariably refers to a deity imaged and conceptualized in male form, this word is judged by some feminist thinkers to be a generically masculine form of naming divine reality, and thus not capable of expressing the fullness of feminist insight....

The dilemma of the word God itself, however, is a real one and not easily resolved....

Why Female Symbols of God?

Normative speech about God in metaphors that are exclusively, literally, and patriarchally male is the real-life context for this study. As a remedy some scholars and liturgists today take the option

Elizabeth Johnson, "Basic Linguistic Options; God, Women, Equivalence . . ." From *She Who Is*. Crossroad Publishing Company. Reprinted with permission of the author.

of always addressing God simply as "God." This has the positive result of relieving the hard androcentrism of ruling male images and pronouns for the divine. Nevertheless, this practice, if it is the only corrective engaged in, is not ultimately satisfactory. Besides employing uncritically a term long associated with the patriarchal ordering of the world, its consistent use causes the personal or transpersonal character of holy mystery to recede. It prevents the insight into holy mystery that might occur were female symbols set free to give rise to thought. Most serious of all, it papers over the problem of the implied inadequacy of women's reality to represent God.

The holy mystery of God is beyond all imagining. In his own epistemological categories Aquinas's words still sound with the ring of truth in this regard:

> Since our mind is not proportionate to the divine substance, that which is the substance of God remains beyond our intellect and so is unknown to us. Hence the supreme knowledge which we have of God is to know that we do not know God, insofar as we know that what God is surpasses all that we can understand of him [the "him," so easily assumed, being the problem that this book is addressing].

The incomprehensibility of God makes it entirely appropriate, at times even preferable, to speak about God in nonpersonal or suprapersonal terms. Symbols such as the ground of being (Paul Tillich), matrix surrounding and sustaining all life (Rosemary Ruether), power of the future (Wolfhart Pannenberg), holy mystery (Karl Rahner), all point to divine reality that cannot be captured in concepts or images. At the same time God is not less than personal, and many of the most prized characteristics of God's relationship to the world, such as fidelity, compassion, and liberating love, belong to the human rather than the nonhuman world. Thus it is also appropriate, at times even preferable, to speak about God in personal symbols.

Here is where the question of gender arises. Given the powerful ways the ruling male metaphor has expanded to become an entire metaphysical worldview, and the way it perdures in imagination even when gender-neutral God-language is used, correction of androcentric speech on the level of the concept alone is not sufficient. Since, as Marcia Falk notes, "Dead metaphors make strong idols," other images must be introduced which shatter the exclusivity of the male metaphor, subvert its dominance, and set free a greater sense of the mystery of God.

One effective way to stretch language and expand our repertoire of images is by uttering female symbols into speech about divine mystery. It is a complex exercise, not necessarily leading to emancipatory speech. An old danger that accompanies this change is that such language may be taken literally; a new danger lies in the potential for stereotyping women's reality by characterizing God simply as nurturing, caring, and so forth. The benefits, however, in my judgment, outweigh the dangers. Reorienting the imagination at a basic level, this usage challenges the idolatry of maleness in classic language about God, thereby making possible the rediscovery of divine mystery, and points to recovery of the dignity of women created in the image of God.

The importance of the image can hardly be overstated. Far from being peripheral to human knowing, imaginative constructs mediate the world to us. As is clear from contemporary science, literature, and philosophy this is not to be equated with things being imaginary but with the structure of human knowing, which essentially depends upon paradigms to assemble data and interpret the way things are. We think via the path of images; even the most abstract concepts at root bear traces of the original images which gave them birth. Just as we know the world only through the mediation of imaginative constructs, the same holds true for human knowledge of God. Without necessarily adopting Aquinas's epistemology we can hear the truth in his observation:

> We can acquire the knowledge of divine things by natural reason only through the imagination; and the same applies to the knowledge given by grace. As Dionysius says, "it is impossible for the divine ray to shine upon us except as screened round about by the many colored sacred veils."

Images of God are not peripheral or dispensable to theological speech, nor, as we have seen, to ecclesial and social praxis. They are crucially important among the many colored veils through which divine mystery is mediated and by means of which we express relationship in return.

The nature of symbols for divine mystery is rather plastic, a characteristic that will serve this study well. According to Tillich's well-known analysis, symbols point beyond themselves to something else, something moreover in which they participate. They open up levels of reality which otherwise are closed, for us, and concomitantly open up depths of our own being, which otherwise would remain untouched. They cannot be produced intentionally but grow from a deep level that Tillich identifies as the collective unconscious. Finally, they grow and die like living beings in relation to their power to bear the presence of the divine in changing cultural situations. In the struggle against sexism for the genuine humanity of women we are today at a crossroads of the dying and rising of religious symbols. The symbol of the patriarchal idol is cracking, while a plethora of others emerge. Among these are female symbols for divine mystery that bear the six characteristics delineated above. Women realize that they participate in the image of the divine and so their own concrete reality can point toward this mystery. Use of these symbols discloses new depths of holy mystery as well as of the community that uses them. Women's religious experience is a generating force for these symbols, a clear instance of how great symbols of the divine always come into being not simply as a projection of the imagination, but as an awakening from the deep abyss of human existence in real encounter with divine being.

The symbol gives rise to thought. With this axiom Paul Ricoeur points to the dynamism inherent in a true symbol that participates in the reality it signifies. The symbol gives, and what it gives is an occasion for thinking. This thought has the character of interpretation, for the possibilities abiding in a symbol are multivalent. At the same time, through its own inner structure a symbol guides thought in certain directions and closes off others. It gives its gift of fullest meaning when a thinker risks critical interpretation in sympathy with the reality to which it points. So it is when the concrete, historical reality of women, affirmed as blessed by God, functions as symbol in speech about the mystery of God. Language is informed by the particularity of women's experience carried in the symbol. Women thereby become a new specific channel for speaking about God, and thought recovers certain fundamental aspects of the doctrine of God otherwise overlooked. To advance the truth of God's mystery and to redress imbalance so that the community of disciples may move toward a more liberating life, this study engages imagination to speak in female symbols for divine mystery, testing their capacity to bear divine presence and power.

Why Not Feminine Traits or Dimensions of God?

Having opted to use the word God, and to do so in connection with female symbols, there is yet another decision to be made. At least three distinct approaches to the renewal of speech about God in the direction of greater inclusivity can be identified in current theology. One seeks to give "feminine" qualities to God who is still nevertheless imagined predominantly as a male person. Another purports to uncover a "feminine" dimension in God, often finding this realized in the third person of the Trinity, the Holy Spirit. A third seeks speech about God in which the fullness of female humanity as well as of male humanity and cosmic reality may serve as divine symbol, in equivalent ways. Searching the implications of each can show why the first two options lead into a blind alley and why only equivalent imaging of God [as] male and female can in the end do greater justice to the dignity of women and the truth of holy mystery.

Feminine Traits

A minimal step toward the revision of patriarchal God-language is the introduction of gentle, nurturing traits traditionally associated with the mothering role of women. The symbol of God the Father in particular benefits from this move. Too often this predominant symbol has been interpreted in association with unlovely traits associated with ruling men in a male-oriented society: aggressiveness, competitiveness, desire for absolute power and control, and demand for obedience. This certainly is not the Abba to whom Jesus prayed, and widespread rejection of such a symbol from Marx, Nietzsche, and Freud onward has created a crisis for Christian consciousness. But it is also possible to see God the Father displaying feminine, so-called maternal features that temper "his" overwhelmingness. William Visser 't Hooft, for example, argues that while the fatherhood of God is and must remain the predominant Christian symbol, it is not a closed or exclusive symbol but is open to its own correction, enrichment, and completion from other symbols such as mother. Thus gentleness and compassion, unconditional love, reverence and care for the weak, sensitivity, and desire not to dominate but to be an intimate companion and friend are predicated of the Father God and make "him" more attractive. A clue to the use of this approach in an author is almost invariably the word *traits*....

... God is not exclusively masculine but the "feminine-maternal element must also be recognized in Him." God persists as "him," but is now spoken about as a more holistic male person who has integrated his feminine side. The patriarchy in this symbol of God is now benevolent, but it is nonetheless still patriarchy. And while the image of God as ruling male as well as real male persons made in "his" image may benefit and grow from the development of nurturing and compassionate qualities in themselves, there is no equivalent attribution to a female symbol or to actual women of corresponding presumably masculine qualities of rationality, power, the authority of leadership, and so forth. Men gain their feminine side, but women do not gain their masculine side (if such categories are even valid). The feminine is there for the enhancement of the male, but not vice versa: there is no mutual gain. Actual women are then seen as capable of representing only feminine traits of what is still the male-centered symbol of God, the fullness of which can therefore be represented only by a male person. The female can never appear as icon of God in all divine fullness equivalent to the male. Inequality is not redressed but subtly furthered as the androcentric image of God remains in place, made more appealing through the subordinate inclusion of feminine traits.

A critical issue underlying this approach is the legitimacy of the rigid binary system into which it forces thought about human beings and reality itself. Enormous diversity is reduced to two relatively opposed absolutes of masculine and feminine, and this is imposed on the infinite mystery of God. The move also involves dubious stereotyping of certain human characteristics as predominantly masculine or feminine. Even as debate waxes over the distinction between sex and gender, and about whether and to what extent typical characteristics of men and women exist by nature or cultural conditioning, simple critical observation reveals that the spectrum of traits is at least as broad among concrete, historical women as between women and men. In the light of the gospel, by what right are compassionate love, reverence, and nurturing predicated as primordially feminine characteristics, rather than human ones? Why are strength, sovereignty, and rationality exclusively masculine properties? As Rosemary Ruether astutely formulates the fundamental question: Is it not the case that the very concept of the "feminine" is a patriarchal invention, an ideal projected onto women by men and vigorously defended because it functions so well to keep men in positions of power and women in positions of service to them? Masculine and feminine are among the most culturally stereotyped terms in the language. This is not to say that there are no differences between women and men, but it is to question the justification of the present distribution of virtues and attributes and to find it less than compelling as a description of reality. Such stereotyping serves the genuine humanity of neither women nor men, and feeds an anthropological dualism almost impossible to overcome. Adding "feminine" traits to the male-imaged God furthers the subordination of women by making the patriarchal symbol less threatening, more attractive. This approach does not, then, serve well for speech about God in a more inclusive and liberating direction.

A Feminine Dimension: Holy Spirit

Rather than merely attribute stereotypical feminine qualities to a male-imaged God, a second approach seeks a more ontological footing for the existence of the feminine in God. Most frequently that inroad is found in the doctrine of the Holy Spirit, who in classical trinitarian theology is coequal in nature with the Father and the Son. In the Hebrew Scriptures the Spirit is allied with female reality as can be seen not only by the grammatical feminine gender of the term *ruah*, which in itself proves nothing, but also by the use of the female imagery of the mother bird hovering or brooding to bring forth life, imagery associated with the Spirit of God in creation (Gn 1:2) and at the conception and baptism of Jesus (Lk 1:35 and 3:22). Semitic and Syrian early Christians did construe the divine Spirit in female terms, attributing to the Spirit the motherly character which certain parts of the Scriptures had already found in Israel's God. The Spirit is the creative, maternal God who brings about the incarnation of Christ, new members of the body of Christ in the waters of baptism, and the body of Christ through the epiclesis of the eucharist. In time the custom of speaking about the Spirit in female terms waned in the West along with the habit of speaking very extensively about the Spirit at all.

There have been various attempts in recent years to retrieve the full trinitarian tradition while overcoming its inherent patriarchy by speaking about the Spirit as the feminine person of the godhead. When the Spirit is considered *the* feminine aspect of the divine, however, a host of difficulties ensues. The endemic difficulty of Spirit theology in the West ensures that this "person" remains rather unclear and invisible. A deeper theology of the Holy Spirit, notes Walter Kasper in another connection, stands before the difficulty that unlike the Father and Son, the Holy Spirit is "faceless." While the Son has appeared in human form and while we can at least make a mental image of the Father, the Spirit is not graphic and remains theologically the most mysterious of the three divine persons. For all practical purposes, we end up with two clear masculine images and an amorphous feminine third. Furthermore, the overarching framework of this approach again remains androcentric, with the male principle still dominant and sovereign. The Spirit even as God remains the "third" person, easily subordinated to the other two since she proceeds from them and is sent by them to mediate their presence and bring to completion what they have initiated. The direction in which this leads may be seen in Franz Mayr's attempt to understand the Holy Spirit as mother on the analogy of family relationships: if we liberate motherhood from a naturalistic concept and see it in its existential-social reality, then we can indeed see how the mother comes from the father and the son, that is, how she receives her existential stamp and identity from them both within the family. As even a passing feminist analysis makes clear, while intending to rehabilitate the feminine, Mayr has again accomplished its subordination in unequal relationships.

The problem of stereotyping also plagues this approach. More often than not, those who use it associate the feminine with unconscious dreams and fantasies (Bachiega), or with nature, instinct, and bodiliness (Schrey), or with prime matter (Mayr), all of which is then predicated of God through the doctrine of the Holy Spirit. The equation is thus set up: male is to female as transcendence is to immanence, with the feminine Spirit restricted to the role of bearing the presence of God to our interiority. . . .

. . . There is real danger that simply identifying the Spirit with "feminine" reality leaves the overall symbol of God fundamentally unreformed and boxes actual women into a stereotypical ideal. . . .

Unexamined presuppositions about the doctrine of God itself raise a further theological question about this approach. In what sense can it be claimed that God has "dimensions," let alone the dualistically conceived dimensions of masculine and feminine? Such an idea extends human divisions to the godhead itself. It actually ontologizes sex in God, making sexuality a dimension of divine being, rather than respecting the symbolic nature of religious language.

We must be very clear about this. Speech about God in female metaphors does not mean that God has a feminine dimension, revealed by Mary or other women. Nor does the use of male metaphors mean that God has a masculine dimension, revealed by Jesus or other men; or an animal dimension, revealed by lions or great mother birds; or a mineral dimension, which corresponds with naming God a rock. Images and names of God do not aim to identify merely "part" of the divine mystery, were that even possible. Rather, they intend to evoke the whole. Female imagery by itself points to God as such and has the capacity to represent God not only as nurturing, although certainly that, but as powerful, initiating, creating-redeeming-saving, and victorious over the powers of this world. If women are created in the image of God, then God can be spoken of in female metaphors in as full and as limited a way as God is imaged in male ones, without talk of feminine dimensions reducing the impact of this imagery. Understanding the Holy Spirit as the feminine dimension of the divine within a patriarchal framework is no solution. Even at its best, it does not liberate.

Equivalent Images of God, Male and Female

While both the "traits" and the "dimensions" approach are inadequate for language about God inasmuch as in both an androcentric focus remains dominant, a third strategy speaks about the divine in images taken equivalently from the experience of women, men, and the world of nature. This approach shares with the other two the fundamental assumption that language about God as personal has a special appropriateness. Behaviorism notwithstanding, human persons are the most mysterious and attractive reality that we experience and the only creatures who bear self-reflective consciousness. God is not personal like anyone else we know, but the language of person points in a unique way to the mysterious depths and freedom of action long associated with the divine.

Predicating personality of God, however, immediately involves us in questions of sex and gender, for all the persons we know are either male or female. The mystery of God is properly understood as neither male nor female but transcends both in an unimaginable way. But insofar as God creates both male and female in the divine image and is the source of the perfections of both, either can equally well be used as metaphor to point to divine mystery. Both in fact are needed for less in-adequate speech about God, in whose image the human race is created. . . .

Although drawing their predominant speech about God from the pool of male images, the biblical, early theological, and medieval mystical traditions also use female images of the divine without embarrassment or explanation. The images and personifications are not considered feminine aspects or features of the divine, to be interpreted in dualistic tension with masculine dimensions or traits, but rather they are representations of the fullness of God in creating, redeeming, and calling the world to eschatological shalom.

Ancient religions that spoke of deity in both male and female symbols may also be helpful in clarifying the thrust of this third approach. As evidenced in psalms and prayers, male and female deities were not stereotyped according to later ideas of what was properly masculine and feminine, but each represented a diversity of divine activities and attributes. In them "gender division is not yet the primary metaphor for imaging the dialectics of human existence," nor is the idea of gender complementarity present in the ancient myths. Rather, male and female enjoy broad and equivalent powers. . . . Both male and female are powerful in the private and public spheres. . . .

The mystery of God transcends all images but can be spoken about equally well and poorly in concepts taken from male or female reality. The approach advocated here proceeds with the insight that only if God is so named, only if the full reality of women as well as men enters into the symbolization of God along with symbols from the natural world, can the idolatrous fixation on one image be broken and the truth of the mystery of God, in tandem with the liberation of all human beings and the whole earth, emerge for our time.

Options

The linguistic options which guide this study, made with the judgment that they are appropriate and necessary, converge into speech about God using female metaphors that intend to designate the whole of divine mystery. Theoretically I endorse the ideal of language for God in male and female terms used equivalently, as well as the use of cosmic and metaphysical symbols. In actual fact, however, male and female images simply have not been nor are they even now equivalent. Female religious symbols of the divine are underdeveloped, peripheral, considered secondarily if at all in Christian language and the practice it continues to shape, much like women through whose image they point to God. In my judgment, extended theological speaking about God in female images, or long draughts of this new wine, are a condition for the very possibility of equivalent imaging of God in religious speech. . . .

Questions for Reflection on Elizabeth Johnson
1. Why is the word *God* problematic for Johnson?
2. If the holy mystery of God is above *all* imagining, on what grounds can we prefer one set of images to another? How does Johnson's position differ from that form of atheism which denies that we can talk sense about God? From an instrumentalism that uses religion as a political or psychological tool?
3. What benefits does Johnson see as following from the use of feminine symbols for God? Why is it not sufficient to speak of feminine dimensions of God?
4. Is Johnson's argument at bottom a political one? What would Johnson say to someone who finds the employment of masculine images helpful in deepening his or her relationship with God, who does not share Johnson's longing for an egalitarian and liberated society, or who finds masculine images psychologically satisfying? How would she reply to Richard Davis (below)?

On the Fatherhood of God

JULI LOESCH WILEY

Juli Loesch Wiley defends speaking of God as Father and criticizes speaking of God as Mother. The Fatherhood of God, she argues, imposes obligations on both men and society to serve, support, and acknowledge the God-given rights of women and (both born and unborn) children.

A key characteristic of the Holy One of Israel is that Yahweh cares for the husbandless woman and the fatherless child. "The desire of the afflicted You hear, O Lord! You pay heed to the defense of the orphan (*yatom*) and the oppressed."

Yatom is often translated "orphan," but etymologically it is more precisely "without a man," or "the fatherless." The "widow" in Hebrew society was not necessarily a woman whose husband was dead, but a woman bereft, abandoned, or alone; and the *yatom* child was not necessarily a child whose father was dead, but could also be a child rejected—unwanted, unsupported, or unprotected by a father. (It is not hard to see a woman impregnated and then abandoned as a "widow" in the biblical sense, and her child, born or unborn, as an "orphan.")

Israel often had a hard time distinguishing the Holy One from the ever-popular Baals of patriarchal Canaanite society. But Hosea (4:14) puts the difference between Yahweh and Baal succinctly: "What we have made with our hands we will never again call 'gods'; for You are *the one in whom the fatherless find compassion.*"

According to the Psalms, the *resa'im,* the unjust, who are the enemies of God, are defined as those who do not defend the cause of the fatherless child and the woman-alone (Pss. 10:14–15; 94:3, 6; 146:9). This theme is taken up from the very first chapter of Isaiah, where the unjust are typified as those who "are merciless to the fatherless: the plight of the woman-alone is never heeded" (v. 23), and where God's people are told, "Search for justice, help the oppressed, do right by the fatherless, be an advocate for the woman-alone" (v. 17), with the significant warning, "If you refuse and rebel, you shall be devoured by the sword" (v. 20).

The *paterfamilias* in the patriarchal Greco-Roman world had life-or-death power over his entire household. His physical or symbolic paternity implied ownership. The absolute identification of *siring* and ownership was radically undercut by the Hebrew realization that God Himself is in some sense the true Father and protector of every child.

It is the Holy One of Israel who opens and closes the womb. Even the very first child, Cain, caused his mother Eve to acknowledge the procreative power, not of Adam, but of God: "I have produced a child with the help of the Lord" (Gen. 4:1). So the Fatherhood of God did not serve to absolutize the power of earthly fathers. Precisely the opposite: it served to relativize earthly paternity. Fathers had obligations toward their offspring because children were conceived "with the help of the Lord."

When Sarah, Hannah, or (in Luke's Gospel) Elizabeth conceived, it is a triumph of the woman and Yahweh: one is almost given the impression that the earthly father is an instrument and bemused observer of it all.

This theme of God's liberating paternity reaches its apex with Jesus, Who was literally "the Son of God."

(I am reminded of a curious story about a nineteenth-century opponent of women's rights who tried to tell the Christian abolitionist/feminist Sojourner Truth that men were superior to women "because Christ was a man." He received the black woman's arch retort: "And where did your Christ come from? God and a woman—man didn't have nothin' to do with it!")

One could almost say that it takes, not *two* to have a baby, but *three:* a man, a woman, and the Holy Spirit. The woman, too, knows that she is not the maker or owner of her child. In the gripping testimony of a woman witnessing the torture and death of her seven sons (2 Macc. 22–23):

> I do not know how you came into existence in my womb. It was not I who gave you the breath of life, nor was it I who set in order the elements of which each of you is composed. Therefore, since it is the Creator of the Universe who shapes each person's beginnings, and brings about the origin of everything, God, in His mercy, will give you back both life and breath.

God makes a relationship with the child He is forming in the womb from the very beginning. In Psalm 139, the singer envisions himself, an embryo, as a person in the hands of a personal God. "Truly You have formed my inmost being: You knit me in my mother's womb"

(v. 13). God sees this young Hebrew's actions (v. 16) and accepts the child's praises even before birth.

Jeremiah was recognized, not only as person, but as prophet before birth. "Before I formed you in the womb," says Yahweh, "I knew you; before you were born I dedicated you; a prophet to the nations I appointed you" (Jer. 1:5).

What does this mean for us?

First, *the Fatherhood of God in no way supports patriarchy* in the sense of a male right to autonomous power in the household. A man has the obligation to serve, support, and acknowledge the God-given rights of his wife and children, or God Himself will be his enemy and judge.

Second, *the Fatherhood of God imposes collective obligations.* Society as a whole must uphold the interests of single women and provide protection and sustenance to children without fathers, whether those children are born or unborn. A nation which fails to enforce the rights of women and children will perish "by the sword."

Third, *the Fatherhood of God guarantees the rights and dignity of each person* because God wills the particular creation of each and every individual, fashions each one for a purpose, and entrusts to each a vocation. God has a right to see each of these vocations come to fruition. Thus, situations where humans fail to develop their personal gifts (as victims of war and abortion, sexual and racial discrimination, hunger, poverty, illiteracy and ignorance, widespread underdevelopment and the squandering of human potential) are an affront, not just to human rights, but to the rights of God.

"That is why I kneel before the Father, from whom every family in heaven and on earth takes its true name." The human rights of all flow from the Father-rights of God.

Is "God the Mother" Just as Good?

JULI LOESCH WILEY

Feminist theologians have said that they have looked within themselves and seen a feminine spirit. The Hebrew and Christian scriptures, however, tell us of a God Who is the Bridegroom of Israel, the Church, and all of us, men and women alike; and for that reason masculine. Reversing the patterns of infantile dependence, the theology of the Father gives us a masculine figure to love impossibly and struggle with. It also frees all of us the awful weight of being under the Mother, and relieves women of the burden of being God Almighty.

Feminist theologians have said they've looked within themselves and seen a Spirit feminine. If their writings tell the story of their search for the Godhead, then the Hebrew and Christian Testaments are the story of the Godhead's search for them, and for all of us. God's choice image is that He is the Bridegroom: and Israel, and the Church, and all of us, *men and women,* are the Bride.

For all their sensitivity to sex, many of the post-traditional feminist theologians are not sexual enough. Many identify the "female imagination" as being "meditative" and "fertile," and then shy away, almost prudishly, from even imagining natural sex. Some even say their meditations become "fertile" *parthenogenetically*—that is, "not dependent on an external catalyst," as Meinrad Craighead insists.

Craighead therefore abandons the sexual metaphor altogether—as it applies to human beings—and prefers the image of procreating from an unfertilized egg, as do certain insects, crustaceans, and worms—all because she will not bring a male generative act into her inward meditations.

Many feminist theologians believe that women have been withheld from full participation in the Christian mysteries. It would be truer to say, however, that it is only women who are admitted to the Christian mysteries, and that any men who would participate must first become "women." This is because in traditional Christian mystical language *all* souls are feminine. (C.S. Lewis says something to the effect that the whole of creation is feminine in relation to the Creator.)

So it is men, *as men,* who are left out of Christian sexual mysticism. The Prophets of Israel, the Doctors of the Church—drawing upon Paul's writings—and the late medieval mystics, male and female, say we must all be Brides. In this respect, Mary is the model, not only for all women, but for all Christians. Men or women who want to unite with God must become other Marys.

It is males who must change most in the spiritual life. Thus it is *not* that women must identify with God (as Mary Daly would say) but that men must *stop* identifying with Him. We women can rejoice directly in our femaleness; men, on the other hand, must empty out their maleness.

"Ah, but you are confining yourself to the limits of patriarchal imagery" retort the feminists. They make much of the fact that all ancient peoples had pictures of gods and goddesses, and then go on as if, for all practical purposes, one is as good as another. Just scan the Jungian menu (Babylonian and Eleusian, too) and order a la carte. Hence, we get from feminists the image of God as "Immanent Mother."

But this is no biblical view. The Hebrew Scriptures, clear through, are a thousand-year polemic against their neighbors' myth systems. Hebrew writers drew on familiar Middle Eastern materials, of course, but only to "spike" them with Yahwism, co-opting them quite cleverly at times. But adherence to the rival images of the other nations is plainly forbidden as idolatry.

Idolatry is the sin most frequently denounced by the Hebrew prophets; and they linked it closely with their second-most-denounced sin, the oppression of the poor and helpless. The prevalence of novel and popular myths is seen as being so dangerous to the community as to bring about its ethical, and then physical, destruction.

Every created thing is, in some way, a revelation of God; and so any image the artist or poet brings up can have, in the very broadest sense of the word, a "sacramental" significance (in the sense that it is an outward sign through which the Creator acts and communicates). So there can be considerable freedom in symbolic language. But this freedom must be disciplined by core considerations.

For instance: let's say we like the Promethean myth rather than the theme of Jesus' sacrificial death on the Cross. So we redesign the Mass in certain ways so that the obedient Jesus becomes the rebel Prometheus; the loving Father God becomes the irate, cruel Zeus; and the object of human life becomes not worship but tyrannicide. This would be relevant to many an individual struggle; it would be useful to many a political and social agenda; but it would not be the Mass of the Christian *kerygma*.

The Mass is the same sacrifice as the Sacrifice of the Cross. It happened "primordially," in a sense, in that the Word is for all eternity offering Himself to the Father; but it also happened within *historical* time: on Golgotha Hill outside the city of Jerusalem, when Pontius Pilate was governor of Judea. And it has an *ethical* meaning which is not ambiguous at all, but painfully explicit. Jesus was obedient to the Father's will, and rescued us from sin through His death, to show His love. And this—both the obeying and the loving—is just what we must do. Jesus said: take up your cross.

Some feminist rite-makers defend their own liturgical revisionism by saying that we must bravely face the anxiety of "uncertain and ambiguous reality"—which is far easier to take than the offensive clarity of Mass and Cross.

Meinrad Craighead says that her Mothergod has but one law: "Create; make as I do make." Craighead explicitly puts this outside of ethical judgment, asserting that "*anyone* involved in creating *anything* new" expresses the "cosmic female force." She draws us to the clear conclusion that this is beyond the old religious concern with "rectitude"—it is beyond Good and Evil.

Some have called this doctrine of the Sovereign Will "Nietzsche for Girls." Perhaps that's too extreme; it must be admitted that the idea of human perfection through self-expression unhampered by "rectitude" can be very attractive. I think an intelligent group like feminist theologians could manufacture six or seven attractive religious ideas in any given morning, and then invent a sacrament or two over lunch.

But if we grant that this post-traditional mysticism can be attractive—even plausible and useful—we still have not asked the really important question: *Is it true?* Many true things are not necessarily attractive; some true things hardly seem plausible, and, far from being useful, seem potentially troublesome. (Take, for instance, a black hole in space. In fact, take all of them.) And this is my main argument with the feminists' Immanent Mothergod: she has not revealed herself (outside of the devotees' subjectivity) to be true.

Hunger, emotion, duress, hormones, chemicals smoked or ingested, or any number of other factors can produce persuasive subjective intuitions. Some people fantasize hell; others, hamburgers. The fact that they are subjective does not make them false; but that they are attractive does not make them true.

Veronica Leuken of Bayside, New York, says the Virgin Mary appeared to her and said women should not wear pants. I don't say Veronica Leuken is a liar. I say she is mistaken. Any of us could make the same mistake.

Jesus' consistency in calling God His Father is one of the most striking features of His teaching. If Jesus did not have a "Theology of the Father," it's safe to say He had no theology at all. And if the content of His teaching is open to radical change, this would mean one of two things: We're saying that we have more inward freedom than Jesus did (Jesus was limited by His times but we are not). Or, while admitting that we are limited by our culture, we assert that ours is a much *better* culture: that is, twentieth-century American society is more deeply and truly religious than that of Jesus' day.

Either way, we're saying we know more about God than Jesus did.

But rather than assume that Jesus' Theology of the Father, His God-language, is archaic and essentially misleading, perhaps we should ask whether calling God our Mother (while metaphorically interesting) is not actually confusing—sexually confusing.

There's one obvious reason why Jesus called God His Father. It was because God *was* His Father. God was not His Mother: *Mary* was. And this is not metaphorical or allegorical at all: it's just the way it is.

If we are baptized "into" Christ, then we take on the same relationships that Jesus has. God is our Father, others in the family of faith are our sisters and brothers, and Mary is our Mother. This has been the belief of Christians since ancient times.

Going back even further we find that exactly one-third of one verse of Genesis describes God's image as both male and female. Despite its brevity, this is said to be a crucial text: one which flashes a kind of beacon light across seventy-two books of Scripture. For instance, God is portrayed as being intimately connected with feminine things: God opens and closes the womb, and delights in pregnancies; God longs to provide milk and comfort for His people (Isaiah 66). God is full of *rachmones,* the Hebrew word for "loving-kindness" which is derived from the root-word *rechem:* a mother's womb. God loves us with womb-love. It is profound.

Yet never in all seventy-two books of the Bible is God called, personally and directly, "Our Mother." Why? A Father with a Womb hardly seems plausible. Hardly attractive. Hardly, with the present feminist agenda, usable. Yet there it is.

The Hebrew and Christian Scriptures abound with various titles and images for God. The titles include Lord, Wonderful Counselor, Prince of Peace. The images include even animals and inanimate objects, both natural and of human making: a Rock, a Shield, a Fortress, a mother eagle urging on her young. And metaphorically, God is seen as farmer-like, shepherd-like, soldier-like—and mother-like.

But all metaphors, evidently, are not equal. Lambs, calves, and snakes may be equal; yet, while Christ can be the "Lamb" of God, we never call Him the Golden Calf or the Sacred Serpent. Why? Because serious confusion would arise, due to the other associations we have with these animals. So these terms are ruled out.

It seems that, given the prominence of both priestesses and goddesses in the religions of all of Israel's thoroughly patriarchal neighbors (Canaanite, Hellenic, Mesopotamian, and Egyptian), the Judeo-Christian avoidance of "God the Mother" and insistence upon "God the Father" was not a matter of "cultural conditioning" at all. It went against the conditioning. It was *counter-cultural*. It is as if "God the Mother" imagery were specifically considered, and rejected.

Again, why?

I don't know. And I know of no authoritative voice in Scripture or church tradition that tells me *why*. But without claiming any authority on my own, and drawing from my own grab bag of symbolic and psychological notions, I would make a few speculations (other than a bias in favor of Scripture and Tradition) why we theists should want to keep our old God the *Father* anyway.

There's a datum of biology I'd like to lead off with in a tentative way. Procreation requires action that is conscious or deliberate on the part of the male, but not on the part of the female. Hence, a man can have intercourse with a woman who is entirely nonactive—even unconscious or in a coma—and beget a child.

This is, admittedly, an extreme example, but it illustrates a fact that is not social or cultural, but anatomical: the act that begets life is *always* active for the male, but not necessarily for the female. In this sense (if in no other) the male initiates generation.

I simply offer this as a datum, not as the basis for a general and socially pervasive theory of female passivity (which God forbid!). But in terms of choosing natural images—sheer metaphor—this may be relevant to the idea of God's coming, God's active giving, our openness, our "letting God," our patient bearing of what God has implanted: an idea common in Christian mysticism.

With the same tentativeness—merely offering this for investigation—I suggest another reason which involves psychological theory.

Psychologist Dorothy Dinnerstein interprets our prolonged human infancy as a time of strong emotions, physical helplessness, and preverbal frustration directed—almost always—at our mother or female caretaker. Dinnerstein shows that we all have deeply ambivalent relationships with mother figures. We have depended upon them absolutely, and raged against them with infant tears because they were so controlling of every sensate need: milk, touch, comfort. She exhaustively details how we go through stages of feeling "smothered" by our mothers, and by women generally. She emphasizes that the father, the male, is *not* the object of all our fervent need and howling resentment—not in the crucial preverbal months of our infancy—because the man's role in the day-to-day routine care of tiny infants has been marginal.

One of Dinnerstein's main conclusions—a theme found in popular feminist psychology—is that the main project for human maturity is to distribute our strong emotions more equally among men and women. Dinnerstein's prescription is to shift the earliest infant care substantially to men, so that our infant bliss and rage will be directed at men and women equally. Yet she doubts that this can actually be carried out on a wide scale. For 99 percent of the human race it's still mothers and other women who tend the babies, and it's likely to remain so. That's how *we* were raised. Can we be born once again?

Then—still following this theory—we might still compensate for the power of *all* our original "Mothergods" by transferring those emotions to a male figure in some other way.

I'm suggesting—and, ironically, feminist psychoanalytic theory itself suggests—that at this point, the resurgence of God as *Mother* could be disastrous. All our impelling hopes and wild fears, our tearful petitions, and our upwelling resentments would still be heaped upon—who? *the Mother!* It's Mother's fault. It always was. How "liberating"!

Maybe one of the sane aspects of our old "improbable" biblical God is that He gives us, at last, a chance to climb into the womb and be born again, from the Father this time.

The Theology of the Father gives us a masculine figure to love impossibly and struggle with like Jacob; a terrible Papa (not Mama) to reproach and beat with Jeremiah fists.

It frees all of us from the awful weight of being under the Mother, *again*. It relieves our mothers—and all women—of the burden of being God Almighty, so to speak, *again*.

In Defense of the Male Priesthood

JULI LOESCH WILEY

Wiley argues against those feminists who claim that an all-male priesthood reinforces patriarchy by pointing out that the priesthood, properly understood, places the priest in the role of a servant. The priest, following Jesus, does not conform to our cultural stereotype of masculinity. Vows of poverty, chastity, and obedience function as a school of humility, checking male tendencies to be self-aggrandizing, sexually aggressive, and dominating.

My favorite scene in my mental movie of the life of Jesus opens with quick camera cuts from image to image of masculine splendor. Fierce sculptures of mounted Roman soldiers raising their swords, their steeds rearing backward on powerful hind legs, nostrils flaring with the green patina of bronze. A close-up of Hannibal engraved on a medallion or a gold coin, brandishing a plumed spear and astride an elephant. Caesars in marble, leading the ranks of the victory march, a bas-relief of infantry, cavalry, captives, slaves. Drumbeats and clarion calls to battle and glory ring in the background.

The camera then swings from this martial and equestrian statuary to a little cloud of dust far off in the distance. The brassy trumpets fade out as the cloud nears, and different sounds rise up from the dust: children's voices, laughter, and a rustic Hee-haw.

Jesus enters Jerusalem on an ass.

Jesus, by his very life, commented decisively on the "masculine mystique." If there are things that the leading men of every age tend to strive for—men, I say, in the non-generic sense: not women—Jesus contradicted them. The failures and weak ones scorned by men, He wrapped His arms around them. The status sought by men, He relinquished it. His aversion to wealth bordered on obstinacy. And the reflex of self-defense-by-violence-to-persons He refused point-blank.

Jesus was not chicken-hearted: but the strength of His manhood was a scandalous contrast to what the world expected—and still expects—of manly striving.

"He is a worm, and no man": this comes easily to the lips of those dubious of Jesus' model of masculinity.

Jesus entered the world as a male. But in entering the male role, he turned that role upside down. He was indeed a king, but His crown was a crown of thorns. He was indeed a master, but one who mastered by serving. He was indeed God, but a God who died.

It is in the context of Jesus' maleness, precisely in His image (or anti-image) of worldly manliness, that I can see the priesthood as a potential "sign of contradiction." I propose the following as a possibility: one important reason why the priesthood is male is that the priest must live out, with Jesus, a scandalous definition of what it means to be a man.

It is clear that Jesus meant to institute a servant-priesthood. Consider the very incident around which many of the arguments about priesthood revolve: the Last Supper.

Much is made of the fact that when Jesus instituted the Eucharist, only His Apostles (all male) were present to receive His command: "Do this in memory of Me."

It is well that they do. In the natural order, it is woman, and woman alone, who can say, "My body is food indeed, and my blood is drink indeed." In the literal sense, in pregnancy and lactation, a woman's body is nourishment to the unborn or unweaned child. Every human being who has ever lived has already experienced a human body, hungered for a human body, as food: the body of the mother.

In our primordial memories, we must all identify womanness that way. And it is a very common thing for us women to identify ourselves that way—as food for others—whether or not our wombs ever carry a baby or our breasts nurse a baby. We feel ourselves to be nurturers.

Even in the intimacy of human love, there is this surging sense of altruism, of self-donation: we feel the impulse to offer ourselves to somebody who is "hungry."

It is just this inner experience that "I, myself, am a banquet," this maternal overflow, which Christ pours out in the Eucharist: "Take and eat: this is My Body." And when he says to His Apostles, all male, "Do this," what is He saying but that men, men above all, must learn to be what women in some obscure sense have always known ourselves to be: bread. A living sacrifice.

Another act during the Last Supper—the washing of the Apostles' feet—seems significant in the same way. In the Palestine of Jesus' day, the washing of feet was a task performed not by a servant merely, but most often by a maidservant. And for the poorer man, coming home from a long day's work, there was a nice wifely feeling to foot-washing, I imagine, like Blondie fetching the paper and the slippers for Dagwood.

This helps us better understand the scandal when Mary Magdalene washed the feet of Jesus earlier in His ministry. ("She's being so—familiar. Don't You know what kind of woman she is?")

I like to think that Jesus was so touched by her gesture that He consciously chose to do likewise. The scandal for His Apostles at the Last Supper, then, was not only that Jesus was playing the servant, but that He was playing, somehow, the "woman."

Simon Peter—a man of the waterfront, full of rough language, armed with a sword, a man's man—is markedly embarrassed. Jesus, who "knew the kind of men He chose," says, "You may not realize what I am doing . . . but if I do not wash you, you will have no share in My heritage." Peter's loyalty overcomes his indignation over Jesus' unseemly behavior; and Jesus makes clear, after He washes Peter's feet, "I give you this as an example: what I have done, you must do."

Men, take note. Is it indisputable that if Jesus is establishing a priesthood at the Last Supper, He is establishing a servant priesthood. There is not the slightest indication that becoming a priest should be a step up on the social or professional ladder: there is every indication that it should be a step down.

This lesson is sharp as a finger in the eye, and Jesus repeats it time after time in blunt language. He directs His men to observe little children as examples of what it means to be great (see Matt. 18:1–7). He describes explicitly how the worldlings exercise their authority ("their great men make their importance felt") and then flings out a flat prohibition: "It shall not be so with you" (Matt. 20:25–26).

It is quite conceivable that one reason why Jesus instituted a special sacrament—holy orders—"just for the men" was that, as Jesus Himself said, "it is not the healthy who need the Doctor, but the sick."

The theologian Valerie Saiving suggests that the attitudes and actions commonly identified with "sin"—self-assertion, will-to-power, treating others as objects rather than as persons—were temptations of men as men in patriarchal cultures: they were not necessarily temptations of women as women.

Saiving does not claim that women are incapable of sinning in these ways. But she suggests that the commonest deadly sins of the feminine character structure may be "triviality, destructibility, and diffuseness; lack of an organizing center or focus; dependence on others for one's moral decision-making," and so forth. In short, a blameworthy underdevelopment of the self.

But because the most stubborn temptations of the masculine character structure are self-absorption and self-promotion, the man who would be virtuous urgently needs to identify with Christ in "emptying himself out." The ascending ranks of bishop-cardinal-pope may have obscured the priesthood's characteristics of self-effacing servanthood. The priesthood has come to be seen (and to be coveted, by some women, and by some men, perhaps, as well) as a bastion of privilege. I propose that it is meant to be a school of humility.

If Jesus Christ had been a woman, the message of self-donating love for others would scarcely have been the scandal that it is. ("Well sure," Rousseau, Freud, and my uncle Frank would say to Her: "You wonderful women are here to help us.") That Jesus was a male is significant; it has a deep and enduring sign-value: Christian servanthood needs to be learned, especially by men. And so, the male priesthood has an enduring sign-value as well.

This school of humility for priests—as models for laymen and women, but especially men—comes most clearly in the religious orders vowed to poverty, chastity, and obedience. These are three great axes laid to the three deep roots of the masculine mystique: the drive for success with money, success with women, and success with power. (Some few priests, alas, don't mind giving up women if they can bed down with money and power.)

We should also note that, traditionally, no priest or member of a religious order was permitted to bear arms. In her classic novel *Kristin Lavransdatter*, set in the fourteenth century, Sigrid Undset has one of her characters exclaim at the great sacrifice of priests in giving up not women (!), but the pleasures of arms and war. Add to that Pope John Paul II's directive that priests should not hold political office, and you have a picture not of clerical power but of a most Christ-like and manly powerlessness.

Priestly power: the less powerful it is, the more priestly it is. The priest is the icon of Christ, but just as we must be able to see Christ's maleness in the priest, so too must we be able to see Christ's humility in the priest.

Postscript 2018

"In Defense of the Male Priesthood," which I wrote thirty-five years ago, still makes, I think, a valid point. It is not at all clear that Christ wants a female priesthood, but we can be certain—heartily certain—that He wants a servant priesthood. In a sense—from a worldly standpoint of money, status, and political influence—the less powerful the priest is, the more priestly he is. That puts a new lens on masculinity.

But strange to say, I don't like this article's snarky, teasing tone about masculinity per se.

As I write now, halfway through 2018, the ascendant version of academic and political feminism increasingly sees manhood itself as a social problem. Anti-masculine views that once were on the fringes of feminism (for example, the S.C.U.M. Manifesto of 1967, which treats the Y chromosome as a genetic defect) have seeped into more mainstream feminism. Masculinity is increasingly viewed as toxic, and boys are pressured to castrate themselves psychologically (and sometimes physically). Because of interactions with our current vindictive, anti-male rhetorical milieu, my article leaves me uneasy.

Having been married to a good man for thirty years and having raised two fine sons who are now adult men, I have come to appreciate masculinity as a gift and as a task.

Masculinity and femininity have an ineradicable impact on identity and calling, and men are not called—not called by God—to be female impersonators. The masculine voice is not the problem, and transposing all the scores in the soprano range is not the solution.

One can still be a patriarch in the Church: but a patriarch reformed by the Gospel. One can be a feminist in the Church: a feminist reformed by the Gospel. "Do not conform yourselves to this age but be transformed by the renewal of your mind, that you may discern what is the will of God, what is good and pleasing and perfect" (Rom. 12:2).

The priest is masculine. The Church is feminine. What matters is not "woman" or "man." What matters, ultimately, is transformation.

Questions for Reflection on Juli Loesch Wiley

1. How does Wiley believe that the Hebrew understanding of the Fatherhood of God had the effect of limiting the power of earthly fathers? How does she see the Fatherhood of God as guaranteeing the rights and dignity of each person?
2. Wiley argues that in relationship with God, "women can rejoice directly in our femaleness; men, on the other hand, must empty out their maleness." Carol Christ says that if we think of God as male, women can see themselves as like God only by denying their own sexual identity. Are they disagreeing? Or are they talking about different phenomena?
3. Why, according to Wiley, does feminist psychoanalytic theory suggest that the resurgence of God as Mother could be disastrous? How would Christ, Ruether (below), and Johnson reply?
4. Has Wiley persuaded you that thinking of God as "Father" does not support patriarchy? Why or why not?
5. Is Wiley hostile to masculinity as such? Is she arguing that Jesus was effeminate and priests should be likewise?
6. Does a servant priesthood mean that the priest should never exercise authority, or even excommunicate an unrepentant sinner?
7. Can women sin in some of the same ways men do? If so, does that make a difference for Wiley's argument?

8. Sometimes women decide that, to get ahead in the world, they have to be as ruthless as men (and are often more so). Does this fact undermine Wiley's argument?
9. Is being poor and powerless a guarantee of virtue, in a priest or anyone else?

Making Inclusive Language Inclusive

A Christian Gay Man's View

RICHARD DAVIS

Richard Davis points out that "inclusive language" excludes male symbols, male images, and male pronouns from the common worship of the Christian community. Many male homosexuals, in particular, feel hurt and betrayed by a language that has often neuterized or feminized God, forbidding Him ever to be Father, Lord, or King.

Some Christians are dead set against any change whatsoever in the language of worship. But few contemporary Christians are so hidebound. Most of us welcome language that more satisfactorily expresses the fullness of our experience of God. Scripture and Christian tradition contain a rich variety of images and symbols that have been employed to speak about God—and not only anthropomorphic ones like Father or Mother, but also images like Rock, Water, Light, Word, Wind, Silence, Mountain, Lamb, Bread, and Wine. Introducing a wider range of images into the common worship of the Christian community would give us a richer and fuller experience of the Being of God, and provide worshippers the freedom to enter more deeply into an intimate, personal relationship with God. Unfortunately, however, much of what goes by the name of "inclusive language" involves *ex*cluding all masculine images and symbols for God and not just including others. The masculine pronoun is eliminated when referring to God and replaced either with feminine pronouns or by the monotonous repetition of the sexless word *God*. Yet we see no rush to replace the numerous feminine pronouns for God in the Book of Wisdom with a monotonous repetition of the sexless word *God*. Have our notions of God advanced only so far as to eliminate our male anthropomorphic images and not our female ones?

Richard Davis. "Making Inclusive Language Inclusive: A Christian Gay Man's View." An earlier version of this article appeared in the newsletter of the *Personage*, a lesbian and gay ministry of the Episcopal Diocese of California. It has been rewritten for this volume. Used with permission of the author.

Many men feel hurt and betrayed by a language that was supposedly created to include us all in a fuller and richer experience of worship, but which, instead, has neuterized or feminized God, forbidding Him ever to be Father, Lord, King, or any other masculine image. Many men have profoundly experienced the feminine in God and wish to express that experience in worship. However, other men wish to affirm their positive image of God as Father, Brother, Coach, Masculine Lover. How can a language that deliberately excludes the masculine be called "inclusive"?

First of all, in the name of truthful scholarship, we ought not to tamper with Scripture. Where the original languages have a particular sexual pronoun, to change that pronoun in English to the opposite sex or to a neuter, or to systematically refuse to translate the pronoun, is censorship. The lesbian and gay community has always been especially sensitive to the issue of censorship because the literature and history of our foremothers and forefathers has frequently been systematically censored to conform to a heterocentric concept of society. Masculine and feminine pronouns in poetry and other works have been played with by heterosexual scholars to create heterosexual expressions of love out of works by lesbian and gay authors. We rightfully condemn such heterocentric bowdlerizations of our heritage. So also should we condemn any attempt to censor Scripture or the language of worship to make it conform to preconceived ideological notions about the nature of God. If Scripture is understood as God's self-revelation, we ought to preserve the rich variety of images and symbols found in it; we cannot do justice to the full Being of God if we refuse to ever acknowledge him in masculine-gendered terms. Despite the enforced gender neutrality of American society, perhaps male and female are two very different, but complementary expressions of what it means to be human. God created us in his image both male and female (Genesis 1:27), and when God wishes to express his Being in a way that is analogous to a peculiarly masculine form, such as Father, then that form must be masculine to be true to who God is. Mother and Father are not mutually interchangeable images, equal to each other in meaning or significance. And the fact that Jesus taught his disciples to call God "Father" provides an additional reason for retaining this way of speaking and thinking about God.

Where central doctrines such as the Trinity are involved, again we should be careful about ill-thought-out experiments in inclusive language. Unfortunately, the level of doctrinal knowledge and understanding is frequently so limited among contemporary Christians that the profound theological significance of an innovative language formula may pass lightly by. It seems to work okay and nobody worries that it may imply a change in credal affirmations! For example, the substitution of the formula "God the Creator, God the Redeemer, and God the Sanctifier" for "God the Father, God the Son, and God the Holy Spirit" on first sight seems to be theologically sound, and it has a nice ring. Yet it reduces God to His functions and moves our attention away from His Being, His *personalness*. Moreover, does this formula imply that

God exists in modalities of function or as successive immanences in human history—both heresies? Perhaps, perhaps not, but I've never heard anyone worry themselves with examining what this inclusive language formula implies about the Being of God.

Often the introduction of inclusive language formulas is motivated not by a desire to experience the God of our fathers and mothers in faith in a richer and fuller way, but by a feminist political agenda. Some materialist feminists see religion and its language as mere tools of the patriarchal social structure. Their primary goal is the restructuring of society at large, and changing the language of worship and the images religious people have of God is just a small aspect of a larger social agenda. They are not interested in God per se but in God as the projected symbol of power structures in society. Change the language used in reference to God; change the power structures. But when ideology becomes the motivation for liturgical change, the freedom and personalism of the individual's living experience of God will get squashed. How many men have been pressured into praying to "our Mother" or "our parent" when their lived experience of God is as a Dad or a Father? (And although my emphasis in this article is on the experience of men, I am sure that those nuns or other women who think of Christ as their spouse, or the many women who think of God as a brother or as a loving Father, would also find that liturgical language eliminating all masculine images or pronouns would interfere with their freedom to experience God in their own way.)

Sometimes advocates of inclusive language are not merely manipulating religion to serve political goals, but rather seeking to explore non-Christian perceptions of God. It is not uncommon for such people to introduce the worship of the goddess qua Goddess, and not only as the feminine aspect of the God of Christian faith. Various pagan and atavistic rituals and prayer formulas are also frequently adopted in order to explore new forms of faith and concepts of divinity. Some do not look back to archaic gods but wish to introduce a more up-to-date conception of God. The personal, transcendent God of Christian faith seems to them outmoded. They embrace instead a New Age vision of a pantheistic god, immanent in all things, an impersonal force. The Christian community can warmly support such spiritual searches and pray earnestly that those searching will find a deeper communion with God. We also hope to learn more about God through dialogue with people who are earnestly on the path of search. But it is misleading to introduce into Christian worship conceptions, prayers, rituals, and formulas that are not Christian; new and strange gods must not be foisted upon the Christian community under the auspices of inclusive language.

Another thing that is sometimes going on under the cloak of inclusive language is an attempt to sneak in by the back door beliefs about God that are incompatible with our Christian tradition. Many American Christians have a strong emotional reaction against the Old Man in the Sky of former piety. Authority figures are rather passé, and Yahweh Sabaoth is decidedly authoritative. We would love nothing more than to rid ourselves of that cranky old warrior-king and replace him with a cozier, more nurturing—need I say affirming?—Big Earth Mama with a soft lap and ample bosom. Thus "Lord" and "King" are eliminated because they are masculine, but they are not replaced by more neutral images of authority. Authority is identified as masculine and therefore given short shrift by those inclusive language writers motivated to convey a more affirming image of God. Male authority figures are either demonized or laughed at. A feminine image of God is thought to convey something caring and nurturing, while a masculine one carries with it negative associations with domination and aggression. Yet to enshrine this reaction against the masculine in our common liturgical language is to enforce the very gender stereotypes from which inclusive language is supposed to free us.

Which brings me to what is perhaps the most troubling thing about inclusive language—namely that it all too often springs from and reflects an antimasculine ideology. If all male pronouns and images must be excised from our common liturgical language, the clear message would seem to be that to use a masculine image or pronoun is to say something bad about God, whereas to use feminine ones is to say something good. Or at least this is how many men will perceive it. Men in our culture are all too often seen as the perpetuators of the worst in human society—war, rape, eco-pillage, and dominance—while women are portrayed as always caring and sensitive—never aggressive or dominating. Boys, it seems, are always in trouble in school, while little girls are always good. Little boys are made of "snakes and snails and puppy dog tails," while girls are made of "sugar and spice and everything nice."

Ironically, Scripture paints a much less stereotyped image of the feminine. Yes, Naomi is an example of God's loving-kindness toward those who embrace him in faith, even if they be strangers or foreigners. Esther is the archetype of God's providence. In the sacrifice of the daughter of Jephthah we see one of the great archetypes of the sacrifice of Christ for our redemption (Judges 11:29–40). But in the Bible we also find Jael hammering her spike through the head of General Sisera—after feeding him milk and cookies (Judges 5:24–27), terrorist Ma Maccabee inciting her sons to undergo martyrdom in Jihad (2 Maccabees 7), and even the Blessed Virgin Mary is pictured marshalling the Church Militant into battle (Revelation 12).

Because of the profound neglect of much in our scriptural and liturgical tradition, many Christians approach inclusive language simply as a process of cutting out offending male pronouns and images. Well, put away those red pencils! That's not the solution. Instead we need to fully own what already belongs to us as Christians in our Scripture and our tradition. For example, the Warrior-God Yahweh already is Mother Eagle, "watching her nest, hovering over her young" (Deuteronomy 32:10, 11). The King of Israel is already Israel's mother. When Zion says that the Lord has abandoned them, Yahweh replies, "Does a woman forget her baby at the breast, or fail to cherish the son of her womb?" (Isaiah 49:14, 51). In the New Testament, Jesus frequently uses feminine imagery in reference to himself and the Father. In the parable of the lost coin (Luke 15:8–10), God the Father is already imaged as a woman sweeping her house. Jesus, lamenting his rejection by his people, cries, "how often I would have gathered your children together as a hen gathers her brood under her wings" (Matthew 23:37). Just as Scripture is already rich in feminine images of God, so also is the living tradition of our Christian faith. For example, the Council of Seville prayed to God the Father, "who bore us in His womb." One ancient icon of Christ's crucifixion shows him pregnant, heavy with child upon the Cross. In Most Holy Redeemer Church in the gay Castro neighborhood of San Francisco, there is a stained glass window picturing Jesus surrounded by children and above is the symbol of a mother pelican plucking her breast to feed her young. Our sexual stereotypes, like the idols of Egypt, lie broken forever when we embrace the true icons of God already found in Scripture and tradition. The problem with the typical heavy-handed ideological approach to inclusive language is that it destroys the delicate ambiguity of these transgendered images of God.

The untruthfulness of either exclusively male images of God or exclusively female images of God is that God is both and neither. Either masculine or feminine images can be used of God as analogies of His Being precisely because they are analogies. They give us true information about his nature, but ultimately, we see through a glass darkly. When some experiments in inclusive language neuterize God that is perhaps the worst of all, for then we are denied the vivid, concrete image of God as Father, as Mother. When speaking of God using anthropomorphic sexual analogies, the tension of opposites must be maintained.

In one sense, though, inclusive language calls us even deeper into our faith. While we cling to our anthropomorphic images of God, Father and Mother, he refers to himself as Rock, Water, Light, Word, Wind, Silence, Mountain, Lamb, Bread, and Wine. Our religion is human-centered. Might not inclusive language be calling us to open our hearts to all of God's creation, whom also he suffered and died to save? Ultimately, we may have to abandon words altogether. St. Teresa of Ávila, a Doctor of the Church, is best known perhaps for her great works on prayer. Yet when she returned to her sisters after her direct apprehension of the glory of God, she could not speak, there were no images possible. She could only bring out her castanets and dance her vision of pure Being.

Whenever I have used a pronoun in place of the word *God* in this article, I have used a masculine pronoun. My primary experience of God is as a Masculine Lover. To quote the Song of Songs:

> As an apple tree among the trees of the wood, so is my beloved among young men. With great delight I sat in his shadow, and his fruit was sweet to my taste. He brought me to the banqueting house, and his banner over me was love. Sustain me with raisins, refresh me with apples; for I am sick with love. (Song of Solomon 2:3–5)

Or I think of John, the disciple whom Jesus loved who was lying close to his breast at the Last Supper (John 13:23). I do have some strong feminine experiences of God and when I am expressing those I may use a feminine pronoun, but that is not my primary experience and so it would be false for me to use "she" instead of "he." I am faithful to Scripture when I imagine God as my Masculine Lover and it is true to my experience as a gay Christian man that he is so, and I am free in Christ to worship him as such. Genuinely inclusive language allows me that freedom and includes my experience in the common worship of the Christian community. Anything else is not inclusive.

Questions for Reflection on Richard Davis

1. Davis argues that "inclusive language" as is currently practiced is not in fact inclusive at all. Explain his argument for this conclusion.
2. What does he think truly inclusive language would be? What positive role does he accord to feminine language about God?
3. Davis is worried about ideologically motivated changes in liturgical worship. Why? What is the purpose of liturgy for him, and how might politically motivated changes interfere with that purpose?
4. Do you agree with Davis about the crucial importance of accuracy in Scripture translation? How would you handle other linguistic problems, for example, pronouns?

God the Father, God the Mother, and Goddesses

SUSANNE HEINE

Susanne Heine agrees that those with impaired images of their fathers may find that thinking of God as "father" harms their relationship with God, although even they may be able to find in God the good father they lacked, and so find healing. But mothers also behave abusively, so that thinking of God as "mother" is not the solution. The tradition has provided us with many names and images of God, and we should welcome this richness and avoid one-sided identifications. Above all we must beware of the "theocratic shortcut" that appeals to the authority of God to authorize the absolute power of human authorities. Heine also corrects some popular misconceptions about God the Father, God the Mother, and the goddesses in light of the biblical record and the surrounding goddess-worshipping cultures of the Ancient Near East.

The Strict Name of God

Blessed art thou
O Lord our God and God of our fathers,
the great, mighty and revered God,
the most high God,
who bestowest lovingkindness,
creator of the universe . . .
O King, Helper, Saviour and Shield . . .
Thou, O Lord, art mighty for ever . . .
Thou art holy

Susanne Heine, *Christianity and the Goddess*, SCM Press, 1988. Reprinted by permission of the publisher.

and thy name is holy . . .
Cause us to return, O our Father, to thy Law.
Draw us near, O our King, unto thy service,
and bring us back in perfect repentance unto thy presence . . .
Bless us, O our Father,
with the light of thy countenance.

"Lord," "revered God," "King," "Shield," "Father"—that is the way in which pious Jews still address their God in the Eighteen Benedictions: in the morning, in the evening, and on the Sabbath. All these names appear in the Old Testament, and more besides: as warrior hero and leader of heavenly and earthly hosts God annihilates the enemies of Israel (Song of Miriam, Ex.15.1ff.; Song of Deborah, Judg.5.1ff.). He is Lord over all other gods and men, strong and terrible, king, supreme lawgiver and judge, a divine patriarch, who—as a feminist verdict has it—justifies all the evil deeds of the male patriarchs.

God is indeed also Father, although he does not have this name in the Old Testament anywhere so often as might be supposed from a knowledge of the New Testament. But God is a strict father: "Know then in your heart that, as a man disciplines his son, the Lord your God disciplines you. So you shall keep the commandments of the Lord your God, by walking in his ways and by fearing him" (Deut.8.6). "For the Lord reproves him whom he loves, as a father the son in whom he delights" (Prov.3.12). As father God gives his people Israel, or even the individual, ethical instruction, The Torah, the "Law of God."

Nevertheless, the strict God of the Old Testament is not a cruel God to his own people: "The Lord is merciful and gracious, slow to anger and abiding in steadfast love. . . . As a father pities his children, so the Lord pities those who fear him" (Ps.103.8, 13). Indeed, love virtually overwhelms the divine Father: "For as often as I speak against him (= the people), I do remember him still. Therefore my heart yearns for him; I will surely have mercy on him . . ." (Jer.31.20). God the Father has taught his people to walk, taken them in his arms and drawn them to him with "bands of love" (Hos.11.3–4). This is no blind love without criteria; just as God is a father to orphans without rights who gives them justice (Ps.68.6), so God knows that people will always remain children and in need of forgiveness. For is there anyone who with the best will in the world does not sometimes fail others? Who among the mortals can say that he is perfect? No one escapes guilt. Anyone who does not recognize that is regarded as a stubborn sinner; judgment comes upon him. But anyone who has insight and turns in confidence to the Father may be certain of the love and mercy of his heavenly Father.

Thus this God has all the traits of the caring father who is strict but just to his children, especially his sons, in the family of the patriarchate. He brings his children up to obey his law, punishes them and rewards them, loves his children and feels offended if the children do not follow him, if they forsake him or even deny him. He can be furious with them, but he wants to win them back by having mercy on them and looking after them. He does not abandon his children, and they do not get away from him. All the authoritarian features of the paterfamilias, but also the humanly understandable and lovable ones, can also be found in God the Father.

The New Testament is striking first of all for the way in which the name Father is used for God much more frequently than in the Old Testament. Here it should be stressed that the address "Abba" (Mark 1.36; Gal.4.6; Rom.8.15), the word that the small child burbles and which is best translated "Papa," is the basis of a new, intimate relationship of trust in God which is free from anxiety: the Father God, who as Son is equal to human beings in everything (sin apart), who lays aside his exaltation and authority so as not to leave men and women alone even in their dying, creates a new relationship with God. Without doubt these features of the New Testament Father God are striking, and so the favorite parable of the Prodigal Son (Luke 15.11ff.) appears in every children's service or school curriculum. Nevertheless, we should not fail to notice that the names of God which attest his power, superiority, and strength are still there: he is the Lord of heaven and earth, the Lord of all men and women, the king who establishes his rule, the judge of good and evil, and the Father who surrenders his utterly obedient Son Jesus to the minions of the law. The Old and New Testaments cannot be played off against one another. Almighty as he is, God can show his people his shining countenance and lovingly lead them on the way of life; but he can also hide himself, and can be experienced as the absent God: where was God when the tower of Siloam crashed down, burying people under it (Luke 13.4)? The dark, incomprehensible, indeed apparently destructive God, who does not lay aside his strangeness, does not disappear in the New Testament. . . .

Such omnipotence removes God from human understanding; it transcends the power of the patriarchal kings, fathers, and other rulers of the world. This has not prevented these rulers from continually deriving their power from the power of God, from transferring the distance between the utterly other God and humankind to the distance between them and their subjects. The parents are "partners in procreation," we read in a rabbinic text from the sixth century of the Christian era. This participation in the divine power of creation then gives the parents, and above all the father, almost divine authority over the children. . . .

This "theocratic shortcut," which has given its blessing to so much abuse, inhumanity, and violence in history, has been criticized by spiritual and political revolutionary movements since the Enlightenment and has also continually been rejected because of its association with a vehement attack on Christianity and an explicit atheism. Nevertheless, final success has still to come. Anyone nowadays who takes part in the life of the Christian community and its liturgical acts will encounter the biblical texts which I have quoted being used in an unreflective way, in prayers and hymns to the God of the "theocratic shortcut."...

Abused Children

Thoughtful theological literature continually stresses that the Father God and Lord God is not to be understood literally and naively: God is not male and has no sex; names and properties have "only" symbolic significance. But what does "only" mean here? Symbols are very closely connected with reality. Women who go to church must immediately get the impression that male properties are at least more appropriate to God than female ones. In addition, there is the hiatus between theological reflection, which has good intentions, and the means of communication through pulpits and cathedras, which hardly stimulate such sophisticated thinking, but naively hand on what the language of the tradition offers. But naive communication cannot lead to reflective reception.

However, what makes the "theocratic shortcut" of this language of the male God so terrifyingly "credible," false though it is, is the quite direct and personal experience which many women have of the other sex. This begins at the tenderest age. My first encounter with a case of sexual abuse of children by close relatives is now well back in the past. In a confidential conversation at that time, an unmarried middle-aged woman told me that from the age of eight she had regularly been subjected to all kinds of sexual abuse by an uncle for almost twenty years. As a result she had not established any relationship with a man and had been undergoing psychotherapy for some time. She came from a good Christian home and for a long time had been involved in various positions and activities in the church and in the community. At the time I did not believe what she said and took it to be the expression of a suspect state of mind; her psychotherapy seemed to me to be more than justified. I am writing this because I am afraid that such experiences might seem just as incredible to others if they come up against them: the literature on this theme, which is the "best-kept secret," but which is slowly but surely coming to light, shocked me over my reaction at the time. Meanwhile I have come to pay more careful attention to my surroundings and know that such experiences on the part of women are not extreme aberrations, nor are they limited to some "lower level" of society....

In view of such experiences, talk about the Father God and God the Father as the representative of law and order, as the one who loves, who has mercy on his children, becomes sheer arrogance. What else can give rise to the cynical image of a father who refers to the fact that he is a father while raping his daughter: "Don't be afraid . . . I'm your father"?

The Motherhood of God

Many women leave the church in order to have done with Christianity and the church once and for all. Others leave the church in order—grotesque though it may sound—to be able to grapple with Christian belief again. . . .

The strongest statements about the motherhood of God appear in Deutero-Isaiah, the later prophet of salvation in the exilic period (sixth century BC): "Can a woman forget her sucking child, that she should have no compassion on the son of her womb?" And the prophet goes on to greater heights: even if a mother forgot her child: "Even these may forget, but I will not forget you" (Isa.49.15–16). God calls his people together: "Hearken to me O house of Jacob, all the remnant of the house of Israel, who have been borne by me from your birth, carried from the womb; even to your old age I am he, and to grey hairs I will carry you" (Isa.46.3–4). God says to the anonymous prophet whom we call Trito-Isaiah, from the period after the exile, who appears in Jerusalem in the Persian period (c.520 BC): "As one whom his mother comforts, so I will comfort you" (Isa.66.13). In the Book of Job God describes his creative activity with terms from the experiential world of the mother: "Who shut in the sea with doors, when it burst forth from the womb; when I made clouds its garment, and thick darkness its swaddling band?" (Job 38.3–9). The action of mother and father can be limited to the idea of comprehensive parental functions: "Has the rain a father, or who his begotten the drops of dew? From whose womb did the ice come forth, and who has given birth to the hoarfrost of heaven?" (Job 38.28–29).

The pious person snuggles confidently up to his God-Mother: "But I have calmed and quieted my soul, like a child quieted at its mother's breast" (Ps.131.2). When the people murmur on their exodus from Egypt and long for the fleshpots of Egypt, Moses too gets weary of his sole responsibility: "Did I conceive all this people? Did I bring them forth that thou shouldst say to me, 'Carry them in your bosom, as a nurse carries the sucking child, to the land which thou didst swear to give their fathers'?" (Num.11.12). Thus Moses reminds God of his maternal duties. But before his death Moses also admonishes the people: "You were unmindful of the Rock that begot you, and you forgot the God who gave you birth" (Deut.32.18). Once again paternal and maternal features of God are combined in the "parenthood" of God.

God is like a mother bird which teaches her young to fly and takes them on its wings (Deut.32.11; Ex.19.4), like a hen who gathers her chickens under her wings (Matt.23.37; Pss.17.8; 91.4; 37.2, etc.). But the motherhood of God can also be directed aggressively against her own children if these turn away from the mother: "I will fall upon them like a she-bear robbed of her cubs" (Hos.13.8). The mention of rebirth from the Spirit (especially in the Gospel of John, e.g., 3.4–7) evokes maternal associations; the parables of Jesus among other things make use of the realities of a woman's life: the kingdom of God can be compared with yeast which a woman mixes with the flour until it is completely leavened; like a woman and her friends who search the house for a lost coin until she has found it, so God seeks out sinners for them to be converted (Luke 13.20–21; 15.8–10). Some feminist theologians also see in the female gender of words a reference to the feminine aspects of the biblical God. The Hebrew word for the Spirit of God is feminine, *ruach,* and the divine mercy which is constantly mentioned in the texts is also feminine, *racham;* moreover it can be translated in its original meaning "mother's womb." . . .

So we can certainly bring together some feminine features and formulate them as a counterbalance to a long tradition of one-sided stress on the masculinity of God. Nevertheless the question remains whether that is honest and meaningful. There is no doubt that male designations for the divine qualities and modes of action predominate in the biblical text. Accordingly the feminist concerns for a feminine image of God seem a little forced, especially where they use the feminine gender of a word for their arguments. The word "Spirit," for example, has a variety of genders depending on the language. In German it is male, in Greek neuter, in Hebrew feminine; in English, of course, nouns have no gender at all. What does one achieve with this argument when one reflects that in German, for example, power, violence, or greatness are all feminine although in feminine judgment they are very closely related to the character of the male? Nor is that the case only in German: in Hebrew not only is the sword feminine, but also *geburah,* male power.

Moreover it is dangerous and contrary to basic feminist interests when a division of the male and female properties of God give a boost to the usual stereotyping of roles. In addition to childbearing, we find that loving care, oversight, clothing, feeding, and the household are seen as "typically" feminine; justice, law, anger, punishment, and power are seen as "typically" masculine.

The maternal features of God to which some feminists refer belong to that part of the tradition which is opposed to goddess myths and cults: Hosea, Jeremiah, Deutero-Isaiah, Trito-Isaiah, Deuteronomy, the Priestly Writing. It is obvious what they want to say. Why do you need a mother goddess? Yahweh, the father, judge, and warrior hero, can also give birth, breast-feed, care for, and have mercy. Even if a mother left her child, God would never leave his people.

Anyone in search of the Old Testament God as mother will find indissolubly connected with this perspective the one God of heaven and earth and the strict father. That can also be seen in a positive light: male and female, separated here on earth, alien to one another or in conflict with one another, belong together in a totality. It is not God's fault that people have not always understood things like this, but instead use the power and masculinity of God as legitimation for the rule of men over men. . . .

Impaired Experiences of the Mother

Let us try another experiment in thinking. Suppose that the biblical tradition had given us a goddess instead of a god, a mother in heaven instead of a father in heaven. Let us once again take up the remarks of many women who say that their unhappy experiences with their physical father got in the way of their access to a heavenly father, but that they could have trust in a heavenly mother. We would evidently not be human were all this impossible. In the course of the feminist revolution women have discovered their problems with their physical mothers, which are worked out less in open violence than through subterranean psychological pressure, yet prove just as great a burden in adult life. Mothers no longer punish so much with their fists as with an indirect threat of withholding love or indicating that they have been insulted in a way which threatens their existence. Such mothers do send out not verbal but emotional signals: If you do that, you'll kill me. "She hardly ever punished us," wrote a woman about her mother. "She had a worse method. If we had to do something and didn't want to do it, then she would say, 'Then I'll do it myself.'" Daughters complain about being tied to mother's apron strings, about being treated like children, about being put down, about too few good words, about too few words at all. "I never understood her (= the mother); for me she was an authority of whom I was afraid"; "I could never touch her; that humiliated me a great deal"; "She recognized me intellectually but she despised me as a person and a woman in the same way that she despised herself." Daughters suffer from the fact that they feel responsible for their mothers, and already did as children; they feel as it were mothers of their mothers. They get on better with their fathers and feel accepted by them. The reverse is also true. Anything, in fact, may be the case. Mothers also exercise emotional power over their sons, just as sons have to suffer violence in various forms from their fathers. The literature is full of examples....

... Women with bad experiences of their fathers may be helped by the mother in heaven; women with bad experiences of their mothers may be helped by the father in heaven. Again it was in a conversation with women after a lecture that I heard one of them say, "If God is a mother, I'm scared of the resurrection."

Neither the phenomenological selection of feminine features of the biblical God nor the historical-critical quest for the place where these features arose, nor recourse to human experiences of parents, seem to me to take us further. If one reflects on the terrifying variety of possibilities of violence between parents and children, then the "disembodied" and transcendent conception of God as the "wholly other" which is so reviled by feminists takes on power to release us: "Thank God" that God is different from us human beings!

You Shall Not Make for Yourself Any Image

Therefore as a fourth and last stage which can in fact help us out of many contradictions, systematic considerations about the question of God are necessary. I shall start from the statement that God *is* Father. What does this "is" mean? The Jewish-Christian tradition has always excluded physical ideas of procreation. The biblical God is not like Zeus, who occupied himself pre-eminently with begetting physical descendants and thus populated heaven and earth with demigods. The Christian confession of the virgin birth is simply meant to say that the conception of a physical procreation of Jesus by God is as out of the question as is his origin simply from a human being. The main reason why the phrase "conceived by the Spirit (of God)" keeps appearing in the biblical texts is to rule out biological associations: the word "conceived" is never to be understood literally. Nor is the phrase "God is father" to be reversed to become "our (physical) father is God." The effect of Judaism and Christianity is to portray God the creator as the "wholly Other," as the one who is defined as not being a creature.

Feminists have labelled this sexless, transcendent, spiritualized, abstract God who is critical of myth a product of a male consciousness and made him responsible for any drop of blood which human beings have shed in their struggle against other human beings: males, theologians "project" a "divided spiritual principle, the product of the development of patriarchal consciousness, on to the cradle of human culture." . . . The human course toward worshipping God without images is not spiritual progress but development toward a schizophrenic—i.e., divided—mode of human existence. The psychologically healthy person remains fruitfully bound up with his or her world of images. . . .

With the prohibition against images the biblical tradition also rejects all attempts to gain control of God as an "object" that can be manipulated and to claim him for all possible interests. The intention behind stating all that God is *not* is to keep God free from the conditions of finitude, from "contamination with the certainty of the senses," but also to prevent him from being imagined as the other-worldly being who "crouches outside the world" (Hegel), from where he stirs up world history at whim, when he feels like it (*deus ex machina*). Even if only in theory, such a world would be conceived of in as objective terms as this one and could not withstand the critical argument that it was a mere projection. But God is not a "thing" either to see or to touch or to imagine. All that would be "bad metaphysics" (Hegel). Were God an object, then objects would be interchangeable: what you set your heart on is your God, says Luther aptly in an explanation of the first commandment in the Greater Catechism. In that case what would be the difference between God and a good, fast automobile? The loss of either equally drives the "owner" to despair. Only the confession of several gods would offer the chance of complaining about the loss to a heavenly rival. By contrast, the transcendent

God of the Bible is the critical principle which is implemented in the same tradition in an ethical claim: You shall not dominate, kill, exploit. . . . On the one hand feminists like Gerda Weiler, whom I have already mentioned, find quite vehement words for protesting against all possible forms of a claim to power, and on the other hand they accuse the biblical God of rigorist moralism which despises humanity. . . .

In the Fullness of Images

Let us return once again to the personal experiences of individuals with their parents. Against the background of our theoretical considerations neither positive nor negative experiences of a father must establish or damage relationships with a father God. It is clear that positive experiences form the basis of the analogy. The one who is loved by a father can say, "If my father . . . how much more my heavenly father." Let me recall the prophet Deutero-Isaiah (Isa.49.15–16), who talks about a mother like this. Many biblical texts talk about God in this way, independently of the analogies of which they make use. The one who is dominated by a father can say: "Though my father does not . . . at least my father in heaven does!" Is the repudiation of an earthly father to have so much power that it destroys any connection with the father God? Negative experiences can also lead to a longing and a hope for protection by the power of God which is superior to all human authorities. Conversation with women has shown me that that is possible, and that many women gain strength from offering resistance.

Father and mother are not the only analogies in talking of and to God. Not very often, but at decisive points in the Bible, God is the friend: God speaks with Moses face-to-face as with his friend (Ex.33.11); God can be called "friend of my youth" (Jer.3.4); and in the New Testament it is said pointedly that Christians are not servants but friends of the Lord (John 15.15). Abraham is called a "friend of God" (James 2.23) and Luke, the great story-teller, produces analogies in extended parables: God is like someone who does not reject his friend when he asks for a loaf at midnight (Luke 11.5ff.).

Eroticism also contributes to the formation of analogies. God is beloved, bridegroom, marriage partner. The Song of Songs, a collection of cultic love poetry, was accepted into the canon (after many difficulties, but it got there in the end) as an analogy for the relationship between God and people. Each side can complain about the faithlessness of the other (Isa.49.14; Jer.2.2). The analogy of the bride brings us to the New Testament, where the kingdom of God is compared to a wedding feast (Mark 2.19f.; Matt.22.1; 25.1). At the end of days this wedding will be celebrated in great splendor (Rev.19.9; 21.9, 17). But all these analogies are in the dialectic of negation, "God is not . . . ," and the claim which transcends everything,

"God is always more than . . ." That can be done by anyone who has made the effort at analogy without being afraid of the many names and images of God which the tradition has brought together. It is precisely its wealth which makes it appropriate for protecting us from one-sided identifications. . . .

Idols and Whores

"They also built for themselves high places, and pillars, and Asherim on every high hill and under every green tree; and there were also 'initiates' in the land" (I Kings 14.23–24). This charge is made against Rehoboam, the son and successor of King Solomon in Judah. He was not the only one; hardly any king, whether in Judah or Israel, was regarded as being beyond reproach in this respect. Anyone like King Asa of Judah who destroyed these "alien" cults was praised. He had expelled the "initiates" from the land, removed all the idols and deprived his mother of the status of "queen mother" because she had had a statue erected to the goddess Asherah—in the Canaanite pantheon the wife of the supreme God El: "And Asa cut down her image and burned it at the brook Kidron" (I Kings 15.11–13). Jehoshaphat son of Asa completed his father's work by exterminating the "rest of the initiates." And the great cultic reform of King Josiah which—according to the text—he implemented with reference to Deuteronomy consisted in orders to "bring out of the temple of the Lord all the vessels made for Baal, for Asherah, and for all the host of heaven" (II Kings 23.4ff.); he "did away with" the idolatrous priests, pulled down the dwellings of the "initiates" "where the women wove hangings for the Asherah" (v.7) and also destroyed all the places of idols in the land: "And he broke in pieces the pillars, and cut down the Asherim, and filled their places with the bones of men" (II Kings 23.14).

Monotheism was far from being something that could be taken for granted in pre-exilic Israel. Even the few passages I have cited show two things: first, how dominant the Canaanite cults must have been among the people of Israel and Judah, and second, that this domination is matched by the vehemence of the repudiation of these cults by the tradition of a later time. Those who handed it on were of the same stamp as prophets like Amos, Hosea, or Jeremiah before them. Among the idols which fell victim to their verdict were in fact a series of significant goddesses. However, whether a return to them is in the interest of feminists remains to be seen. . . .

The goddess Anat is without doubt the most impressive figure. She fights, wades in the blood of her opponents, is not "sated with her killing; the heads she has cut off reach up to her waist." "She is filled with joy as she plunges her knees in the blood of heroes." . . . Anat acts just like Yahweh, at least when it comes to annihilating her enemies. Why is Yahweh then accused of violence by feminists and not Anat? At any rate it is a sign of progress that Yahweh does not wade with joy in the blood of his enemies. . . .

Since Anat and Baal, like Asherat and El, are gods of fertility, and war is identified with drought, and love and peace with growth and flourishing, Anat's battle may also be connected with this. Anat is always angry when she has to save Baal; then she couples with him, for only together do they create fertility. So Anat longs for Baal "like the heart of the mother sheep for its lamb"; they celebrate their love feast in a meadow, taking the form of cattle, so that Anat bears a calf (cf. the cult of the golden bull or calf). This form of religion is therefore aptly called a fertility cult or vegetation cult: human children, young animals, corn, and fruit are to grow. What happens in "heaven," the expulsion of the gods, their defeats and victories, determines life and death. All eroticism is in the service of fertility. And again a conflict with feminist interests is clear; anyone who is on guard against reducing women to fertility and motherhood can hardly lay claim to the goddess myths. Anat certainly fights, but she fights in order to make all living things fertile. A lack of fertility at that time was probably the worst thing that could happen to a woman. We can see that from the Old Testament. As Sarah does not get any children, she sends her husband Abraham to the maid (Gen.16.1ff.); when Rachel sees that her womb remains closed her husband Jacob has to get children for her through the maid Bilhah (Gen.30.1ff.). The husbands do what their wives tell them, for descendants are of more value than the personal relationship between man and woman. . . .

All this shows how remote is the interest of women of four thousand years ago from what moves women today. Feminists who revive the myths and rites from this period therefore overlook what was decisive at that time. They do not pray to the goddesses for fertility, yet this is the cornerstone of the submerged world of the feminine deities, and the myth, thus robbed of its intention, becomes barren in both the literal and the metaphorical sense. What has it to offer us in a period and civilization for which fertility has become a burden, if not a curse? If the women of those days rose up again, from a time when fertility was overshadowed by the early deaths of mothers and children, and heard our debates over contraception and abortion, our world would seem as strange to them as on close inspection theirs must appear to us. The selection of themes by feminists, when they depict, e.g., Anat as mistress of life and death, when they depict the one set over her mortal hero, the gracious, warlike one who takes the initiative in love, exclusively "proves" their interest. This is what women want to be today; they want to break the tradition of male destructive domination of their body and their soul. They are right. It is high time for that. But the arguments must be different; the arguments derived from the goddess myths can all too easily be turned against those who use them.

Questions for Reflection on Susanne Heine

1. To what extent does the Bible refer to God as Father? To what extent as Mother? What is the attitude of the Old Testament prophets to goddess worship? What implications does Heine draw from these features of the Bible?
2. Why have feminists preferred God the Mother or goddesses to God the Father, and what about their reasons does Heine find unconvincing? (Consider, in particular, her observations concerning Canaanite goddess worship.)
3. What lessons does Heine draw from "impaired experiences of the mother"?
4. What is the theocratic shortcut, and what is wrong with it? How does Heine attempt to avoid it?

Why Christians Name God "Father"

GARY CULPEPPER

Gary Culpepper focuses on the theological issue of how Christians should name the One God in public acts of worship in accord with the pattern established by Jesus' own practice of naming God. For Christians, he argues, Jesus' use of the name "Father" is not simply a "metaphor" drawn from general human experience, but is employed as a name to identify a particular Person whose existence would otherwise be unknown and unknowable apart from the witness of Jesus the Son. Christian belief in the Trinity as a communion of divine Persons who act to make human persons, male and female, partakers in the divine nature is connected to Jesus' unique way of addressing God as "Father." Faithful appropriation of Jesus' practice will, Culpepper argues, exclude the distorted readings that have supported the oppression of women.

The doctrine of God is a principal area of concern in Christian feminist theology today. This follows most obviously, perhaps, for the reason that Christian understanding and worship of God is formulated primarily in terms of nouns (e.g., Father, Son, Lord, King) and corresponding pronouns (He, His) which, in ordinary English usage, refer exclusively to males. To some, this exclusivity stands in the way of women's liberation. To insist upon a tradition which excludes the practice of naming God "Mother" as well, the argument runs, further confirms the complicity of the Christian religion in the history of sexist oppression.

Typically, feminist theologians link a political and sociological criticism of Christian religion with strictly theological arguments to contend that the traditional Christian grammar of speech about God embodies a distorted, "patriarchal" understanding of the nature of divinity. Speech about "God the Father," these theologians contend, supports the belief that God's

Cupepper. 'Why Christians Call God "Father."' Written for this volume.

"otherness" and power are best pictured by an emotionally detached male ruler of the world, a belief which both legitimates male rule over women in Church and society *and* fails to communicate the truth about the intimate, "maternal" love that the Christian God bears for the world.

The issue of how Christians are to address God is complex. First, there are names and/or designations for God—such as Almighty, the Good, or Being Itself—which identify the divine nature in a general way that is open to philosophical discussion. Second, there are names which are more "personal" in their connotation, insofar as they communicate the identity of a "living God" who performs particular saving deeds in history. This "living God" is not discovered merely through philosophical analysis of names such as "the Almighty." For example, the name "God of our fathers Abraham, Isaac, and Jacob" identifies the personal identity of God in a way that the name "Infinite" cannot. In Christian theology, yet another dimension enters into the practice of naming God: names for God can refer to the three divine persons—Father, Son, and Holy Spirit—who are distinct from one another, though exist as One God.

This new dimension in naming God—the belief that God is a Trinity of persons, each with a distinct name—has its roots in the saving revelation of this "three-person God" in the life, death, and resurrection of Jesus Christ. For our purposes, the issue can be focused most instructively upon Jesus' practice of addressing the God of Jewish faith as "Abba," or "Father," and teaching his disciples to do the same. Theologians who support the use of the name "Father" in Christian prayer believe that Jesus' own practice is *more than* merely a product of Jewish cultural conditioning; according to these theologians, the name "Father" is an integral element in the revelation of the three-person God—Father, Son, and Holy Spirit.

Feminist theologians critical of the privileged status accorded the name "Father" in Christian prayer and doctrine today typically do not deny that the practice of naming God "Father" is a distinctive feature of Jesus' life and ministry. This raises what at first seems to be a problem: the historical source of a tradition which is taken to be oppressive of women seems, at first glance, to be Jesus himself, the eternal God Incarnate. Yet certain arguments are advanced by Christian feminist theologians at this point concerning the metaphorical nature of names for God, including Jesus' use of "Father." While the complexity of feminist theology precludes easy generalizations, these arguments have two basic features in common: (1) an affirmation of the incomprehensibility of God, which (2) supports the axiom that all speech about God is strictly metaphorical in character.

The theologian Elizabeth Johnson (whose work appears in this collection) has advanced such a theory of the metaphorical nature of religious language, and she appeals frequently for support of her position to the theology of St. Thomas Aquinas, a thirteenth-century theologian whose contributions are especially esteemed among Roman Catholics. Aquinas taught that the divine nature is truly said to be incomprehensible for human understanding, and acknowledged that metaphors are often employed in Scripture to communicate a real, though imperfect, understanding of God. Unlike Johnson, however, Aquinas argues that there exists a class of non-metaphorical names which are predicated of God, among which belongs the name "Father."

Johnson, on the other hand, employs the doctrine of God's incomprehensibility to support the position that all names for God are metaphorical. In a departure from Aquinas, Johnson argues that God is ultimately "nameless." How, then, are we to justify using any names for God at all? Johnson looks to the practice of Jesus and points out that, while he addressed God as his "Father," we should not overlook the fact that he also proposed female images of God to his audience as well (e.g., the woman in search of the lost coin in Luke 15:4–10).

Since all names for God are metaphorical, according to Johnson, there can be no substantial difference between Jesus' use of the name "Father" for God and the other images, masculine or feminine, he may have employed to communicate the Gospel. Accordingly, Johnson can maintain that the practice of Jesus himself legitimates the use of metaphors drawn from male and female experience alike in our prayerful desire to publicly address the person of God revealed in and through Jesus. Johnson uses her doctrine of the metaphorical structure of religious language to: (1) advocate for a vigorous development and use of female metaphors in our speech about God, that (2) function as *equivalents* to the name "Father," as the latter has come to be used in Christian prayer and doctrine, which (3) will aid in overcoming patriarchal oppression in society. But it is far from clear that (2) is the case when the issue is considered from the perspective of how God comes to be addressed in the history of Jewish and Christian prayer and theology, or that (3) follows from (1) and (2).

Jewish theology affirms that God is One, a Oneness which implies the holiness and transcendence of God beyond the human power to imagine or conceive. The sacred name of the God of Israel is revealed to Moses *neither* as "Father" nor "Mother," but in the words "I am Yahweh" (Exodus 3:14), a name which is variously translated "I am who I am," "I am who I will be," or "I am who causes to be." Jewish consciousness of the holiness of God led further to this name being rendered YHWH (the "Tetragrammaton") in its sacred texts, rendering it unpronounceable in liturgical prayer. From at least the time of the Babylonian exile (sixth century BC), the pronounceable name "Father" came into use in Jewish prayer as a *vocative*, a part of speech employed to address a *particular* someone in order to be heard (as in ordinary usage, "Father, will you help me with my homework?").

The Jewish use of the name "Father" for Yahweh suffers from certain limitations—limitations which suggest that it is properly classified as a metaphorical vocative. This is the case for the Jew, since there is nothing that belongs to the definition of the term "Father" that can, strictly speaking, be said of the God of Israel. First, Yahweh is not male (nor female, nor androgynous), and second, "Father" implies a relation to a son or daughter, and it was the hallmark of Jewish monotheism, in its criticism of pagan polytheism, to deny that anyone or anything enjoyed this kind of relation to Yahweh. Hence, "Father" is metaphorical; the proper, non-metaphorical name of the God of Israel is "Yahweh."

To conclude that Jewish speech about God the "Father" is metaphorical is not to say that this name (as a liturgical vocative) is without theological meaning. Naming Yahweh "Father" in Judaism is not simply arbitrary. It would be a mistake, however, to think that its meaning for the Jew was derived from a general human experience of fatherhood, such that, when said of Yahweh, "Father" should be taken to mean "a being like the male head of the household." This interpretation would overlook the particularity of Jewish history that is the context in which the name gained its concrete meaning, as distinct from the significance of the name "Father" in other Ancient Near Eastern religions.

Among the historical associations which give Jewish use of the name "Father" its distinctive meaning, the figures of Abraham and David enjoy primacy. Abraham is remembered as the father of Jewish faith, an honor attributed to him both because he was the first to enter into the covenant of faith established by Yahweh, and because he accepted responsibility for the transmission of this faith signified in the practice of male circumcision. Metaphorical extension of the name "Father" to Yahweh points out that the authority of Abraham, and the whole of Jewish patriarchal culture, derives from and has its basis in the authority of Yahweh and the covenantal law. So, too, political authority is based not in man but in God. Significant here, especially for Christian theology, is the Jewish understanding of God as the "Father" of the king who presides over the people of Israel as the adopted son of Yahweh, with particular reference to that future king whom the prophet Nathan prophesied would come from the house of David to reign justly and eternally over the nations (2 Samuel 7:14).

Feminist theologians are correct to point out that the use of the name "Father" in Jewish religion is related to a patriarchal form of life. This fact, however, ought not lead one immediately to the conclusion that the exclusive use of the name "Father" for God represents an attempt to construct the image of God as a projection of adult Jewish male desire for unrestrained dominance over women and children. The Jewish prophets railed against idolatrous projection of human experience in religion and rejected the practice of naming Yahweh equivalently as "Mother" in an effort to reinforce Jewish belief that God is not sexually differentiated as male and female.

It was Israel's neighbors who named the divine equivalently "Father" and "Mother" in accord with their polytheistic belief in male and female gods (see Jeremiah 2:20–28). Jewish religion distinguished sharply between created sexual life-forces and the life-force of Yahweh, and employed speech about God the "Father" to communicate that Yahweh is beyond the forms of sexual distinction which occupied the attention of those in non-Jewish religious cults. This does not mean that the use of female imagery and metaphors for God is strictly inadmissible in Jewish religion (e.g., Hosea 11:1–4), but points to the prophetic concern to distinguish polytheistic and monotheistic religious belief and practice.

The Christian theologian, however, notes a difference between Jesus' use of the name "Father" and the monotheistic purposes of naming God "Father" in the Jewish prophets. This is because the name "Father" on the lips of Jesus is understood to mean that there is a distinctive sense in which God is Jesus' eternal Father, and, reflexively, that Jesus is God's eternal Son. The Christian theologian might see things like this: *our* speaking about God as "Father" is merely metaphorical (in the sense that we are not really the eternal sons or daughters of God), but *Jesus'* speaking about God as "Father" is more-than-metaphorical. But if *all* language about God is merely metaphorical, as Johnson insists, then this difference in Jesus' use of "Father" does not really show itself to us. This, then, is the most important theological point in Christian understanding of God the "Father": the name "Father" refers to *the particular Person of God* disclosed in Jesus' personal word and deeds, not to a transcultural "father-figure" derived from generic human experience.

The importance of Aquinas's distinction between metaphorical and "more-than-metaphorical" flows from this concern. All the same, many will be perplexed by the claim that naming God "Father" *dissociates God* from existence as male. According to St. Thomas Aquinas (to whom Johnson appeals for her own doctrine of God's incomprehensibility), metaphorical speech involves the use of a word or image to communicate some truth about the reality of God which, when pressed, will ultimately fail, because the definition of the word is inescapably bound up with the conditions of finitude and lack of perfection. In contrast, Aquinas holds that the theologian will also discover more-than-metaphorical, or "proper," names that are said of God and do not break down or fail, precisely because there exists *some* aspect of the definition of the term which does not communicate finitude or lack of perfection (see Aquinas, *Summa Theologiae* I, q.13, a.3).

Take two propositions which Aquinas himself offers for consideration: "God is our Rock" and "God is the Father of our Lord Jesus." In the case of naming God our "Rock," Aquinas insists that such speech is metaphorical, for bodiliness belongs to the definition of "rock" and hence is properly said of the mineral and improperly said of God (though the metaphor communicates the truth that God is faithful or unchanging in His love for us). The situation is different with the name "Father," according to Aquinas, for the definition of "Father" is not "to be male" but to be the "begettor" or "personal origin" of another, and this relational aspect of the definition of the name "Father" implies neither finitude nor imperfection: in Christian revelation, God is the eternal Father, or "personal origin," of the Son Jesus.

Two problems might be raised against this view. First, is it not the case that both the terms "Rock" and "Father," derived as they are from our experience of the bodily, material world, communicate equally the aspect of limitation? Second, if "Father" is said non-metaphorically of God, does this not violate the doctrine of divine incomprehensibility?

In response to the first problem, Aquinas answers—and this is very important—that the name "Father" is *not* derived from our natural knowledge or experience of the world; rather, it is derived from our hearing the speech of Jesus the eternal Son in faith. On these grounds, Aquinas argues that the name "Father," like all proper names for divinity, is said most truly of God, and refers to our natural experience of fathers and fatherhood only secondarily and by analogy. This sheds light on the meaning of Jesus' command "call no man your father on earth, for you have one Father, who is in heaven" (Matthew 23:9): the name "Father" can be said *truly* of the human male only insofar as the sexual and interpersonal dimension of his existence embodies the perfection of the divine love manifest in Christ (see Ephesians 3:14).

In order to answer the second question about God's incomprehensibility, Aquinas developed a theological theory of language which attempts to clarify how it is that the meaning of a term said non-metaphorically of God is neither identical to (univocal speech) nor radically dissimilar from (equivocal speech) the meaning of the term when used in our ordinary discourse. Aquinas referred to this mean between univocal and equivocal speech which allowed terms to be predicated non-metaphorically of God as a language of analogy.

Theologians who, like Johnson, do not admit to a distinction between metaphorical and non-metaphorical naming of God follow a trajectory closer to that of the Jewish theologian Rabbi Moses Maimonides, a contemporary of Aquinas who insisted upon the radical dissimilarity of the meaning of our words when said of God. Aquinas, whose aim was to explain the name "Father" in the new context of Christian revelation and belief in Jesus as the Son of God, rejected the adequacy of Maimonides' view (see Aquinas, *Summa Theologiae* 1, q.13, a.2). "Divine incomprehensibility" means something very different for Aquinas, who held that we can know by Christian faith *that* God is a Father (of Jesus, his eternal Son), but insisted equally that *how* God exists as Father will remain eternally incomprehensible. Aquinas's doctrine of analogy affirms the incomprehensibility of a God who is knowable to some degree, not that God is completely unknowable.

Of what consequence is this issue for Christian belief and life, especially in connection to the concerns of feminism and feminist theology? An answer to this question might be found in Aquinas's argument that the name "Father," when spoken by Jesus, reveals that God is the trinity of persons whose existence would otherwise be unknown and unknowable apart from the living witness of Jesus the Son. The Trinity is the central mystery of salvation for Christians, for it discloses that divine life is the existence of distinct persons dwelling in love without subordination of one to another. Christians understand salvation to be an entrance into personal communion with the Trinity of divine persons, not as slaves subordinated to an all-powerful male divinity, but in a relation of friendship with the One God, neither male nor female. Theologians who affirm only the possibility of metaphorical speech about God undermine this central mystery of Christian religion, for metaphorical language is always bound up with limitation and hence cannot be said to capture the truth about God. But the Christian believes that "Father" *is* said truly of God, precisely in the sense that this name refers to that person who begets and in turn sends his eternal Son to offer humanity the fullness of divine life. Johnson's argument that all theological language is metaphorical has the effect of erasing or obscuring the particularity of the God revealed by Jesus, which in turns reduces "God" to a generic human construct that evokes human criticism and reconstruction. Johnson's experiment in the reconstruction of Christian language for God has not been received or appropriated as a fruitful contribution to the life of the Christian Church. The work of more recent feminist theologians, such as Sarah Coakley's *God, Sexuality, and the Self* (2013), explores ways in which the particularity of the God of Jesus Christ, the "Father," is a source of liberation and salvation for women and other marginalized persons.

At the end of this essay, which has attempted to argue that the use of the name "Father" for God in the Christian religion ought to point our attention not to yet another ideological construct of a patriarchal culture, but to the liberation offered by the Son to men and women alike, the question might still remain: Why is it that the name "Mother" cannot be said non-metaphorically of God as well? While there has been much discussion of whether, from a sexual/biological point of view, the name "Father" more perfectly captures the sense of "personal origin" than "Mother," that debate need not occupy our attention here. This is so because the names which the Christian uses for God are not derived from philosophical reflection, political or social experience, or biology, but from the personal relations manifest in the life of Jesus, the Son of God. The revelation of God in the life of Jesus and his personal relations leads one to understand that "Mother" is said non-metaphorically, not of God, but of Mary, the Mother of Jesus, whose receptivity to divine grace establishes her as the true Mother of God and the spiritual Mother of all Christians.

This differentiation in the use of the names "Father" and "Mother" inscribed in the very pattern of Jesus' own life relations and anticipated by the use of "Father" in Jewish religion will, sadly, continue to offer the occasion for the development of distorted patriarchal interpretations of the relations of the sexes. This essay has attempted to argue that (1) such distortions are not the result of a faithful appropriation of these religious traditions, and (2) there does not exist any evidence, in the history of religions or otherwise, that a modification of this Christian pattern of naming God in prayer and theology will bring about the sort of liberation of women described in Christian feminist theology. Something more must be said, however: the practice of naming God "Father," in the spirit of Christian faith, directs our lives toward greater conformity to Jesus the Son, who offered himself in life and death so that Jew and Greek, slave and free, male and female (cf. Galatians 3:28) will live as reconciled to one another in the God who is Father, Jesus the Son, and the Holy Spirit.

Questions for Reflection on Gary Culpepper

1. Explain the difference between metaphorical and proper uses of language when speaking of God. How can calling God *Father* be non-metaphorical if we do not believe that God has a male body?
2. According to Culpepper, what difference does it make that Jesus frequently called God *Father?* What is the role of the doctrine of the Trinity in his argument?
3. Why can't both *Mother* and *Father* be used of God, since God is by common consent above all concepts?

Ecofeminism

Symbolic and Social Connections of the Oppression of Women and the Domination of Nature

ROSEMARY RADFORD RUETHER

Ecofeminism, Rosemary Radford Ruether explains, represents the union of the radical ecology movement and feminism. She argues that thinking of God as single, male, and transcendent has been used to justify human exploitation of nature and patriarchal denigration and oppression of women. She calls for a new ecofeminist culture and ethic, in which all racist, classist, cultural, and anthropocentric assumptions of superiority and inferiority will be discarded. Among other things, this means allowing women more access to public culture, and converting males to an equal share in the tasks of child nurture and domestic maintenance.

…Ecofeminism represents the union of the radical ecology movement, or what has been called "deep ecology," and feminism. The word "ecology" emerges from the biological science of natural environmental systems. It examines how these natural communities function to sustain a healthy web of life and how they become disrupted, causing death to plant and animal life. Human intervention is obviously one of the main causes of such disruption. Thus ecology emerged as a combined socioeconomic and biological study in the late sixties to examine how human use of nature is causing pollution of soil, air, and water, and destruction of the natural systems of plants and animals, threatening the base of life on which the human community itself depends.

Deep ecology takes this study of social ecology another step. It examines the symbolic, psychological, and ethical patterns of destructive relations of humans with nature and how to replace this with a life-affirming culture.

Ruether from *Ecofeminism and the Sacred*, edited by Carol J. Adams. 1993. Continuum Publishing Company. Reprinted by permission of Continuum International Publishing Company, Inc.

Feminism also is a complex movement with many layers. It can be defined as only a movement within the liberal democratic societies for the full inclusion of women in political rights and economic access to employment. It can be defined more radically in a socialist and liberation tradition as a transformation of the patriarchal socioeconomic system, in which male domination of women is the foundation of all socioeconomic hierarchies.

Feminism can be also studied in terms of culture and consciousness, charting the symbolic, psychological, and ethical connections of domination of women and male monopolization of resources and controlling power. This third level of feminist analysis connects closely with deep ecology. Some would say that feminism is the primary expression of deep ecology....

... What I plan to do in this essay is to trace some symbolic connections of domination of women and domination of nature in Mediterranean and Western European culture. I will then explore briefly the alternative ethic and culture that might be envisioned, if we are to overcome these patterns of domination and destructive violence to women and to the natural world.

Pre-Hebraic Roots

Anthropological studies have suggested that the identification of women with nature and males with culture is both ancient and widespread. This cultural pattern itself expresses a monopolizing of the definition of culture by males. The very word "nature" in this formula is part of the problem, because it defines nature as a reality below and separated from "man," rather than one nexus in which humanity itself is inseparably embedded. It is, in fact, human beings who cannot live apart from the rest of nature as our life-sustaining context, while the community of plants and animals both can and, for billions of years, did exist without humans. The concept of humans outside of nature is a cultural reversal of natural reality.

How did this reversal take place in our cultural consciousness? One key element of this identification of women with nonhuman nature lies in the early human social patterns in which women's reproductive role as childbearer was tied to making women the primary productive and maintenance workers. Women did most of the work associated with child care; food production and preparation; production of clothing, baskets, and other artifacts of daily life; cleanup; and waste-disposal.

Although there is considerable variation of these patterns cross-culturally, generally males situated themselves in work that was both more prestigious and more occasional, demanding bursts of energy, such as hunting larger animals, war, and clearing fields, but allowing them more space for leisure. This is the primary social base for the male monopolization of culture, by which men reinforced their privileges of leisure, the superior prestige of their activities, and the inferiority of the activities associated with women.

Perhaps for much of human history, women ignored or discounted these male claims to superiority, being entirely too busy with the tasks of daily life and expressing among themselves their assumptions about the obvious importance of their own work as the primary producers and reproducers. But, by stages, this female consciousness and culture were sunk underneath the growing male power to define the culture for the whole society, socializing both males and females into this male-defined point of view.

It is from the perspective of this male monopoly of culture that the work of women in maintaining the material basis of daily life is defined as an inferior realm. The material world itself is then seen as something separated from males and symbolically linked with women. The earth, as the place from which plant and animal life arises, became linked with the bodies of women, from which babies emerge. . . .

The conquest and enslavement of other tribal groups created another category of humans, beneath the familiar community owned by it, whose labor is coerced. Enslavement of other people through military conquest typically took the form of killing the men and enslaving the women and their children for labor and sexual service. Women's work becomes identified with slave work. The women of the family are defined as a higher type of slave over a lower category of slaves drawn from conquered people. In patriarchal law, possession of women, slaves, animals, and land all are symbolically and socially linked together. All are species of property and instruments of labor, owned and controlled by male heads of family as a ruling class.

As we look at the mythologies of the Ancient Near Eastern, Hebrew, Greek, and early Christian cultures, one can see a shifting symbolization of women and nature as spheres to be conquered, ruled over, and finally, repudiated altogether.

In the Babylonian creation story, which goes back to the third millennium B.C.E., Marduk, the warrior champion of the gods of the city states, is seen as creating the cosmos by conquering the Mother Goddess Tiamat, pictured as a monstrous female animal. Marduk kills her, treads her body underfoot, and then splits it in half, using one half to fashion the starry firmament of the skies, and the other half the earth below. The elemental mother is literally turned into the matter out of which the cosmos is fashioned (not accidentally, the words *mother* and *matter* have the same etymological root). She can be used as matter only by being killed—that is, by destroying her as "wild," autonomous life, making her life-giving body into "stuff" possessed and controlled by the architect of a male-defined cosmos.

The Hebraic World

The view of nature found in Hebrew Scripture has several cultural layers. But the overall tendency is to see the natural world, together with human society, as something created, shaped, and controlled by God, a God imaged after the patriarchal ruling class. The patriarchal male is entrusted with being the steward and caretaker of nature, but under God, who remains its ultimate creator and Lord. This also means that nature remains partly an uncontrollable realm that can confront human society in destructive droughts and storms. These experiences of nature that transcend human control, bringing destruction to human work, are seen as divine judgment against human sin and unfaithfulness to God (see Isaiah 24).

God acts in the droughts and the storms to bring human work to naught, to punish humans for sin, but also to call humans (that is, Israel) back to faithfulness to God. When Israel learns obedience to God, nature in turn will become benign and fruitful, a source of reliable blessings, rather than unreliable destruction. Nature remains ultimately in God's hands, and only secondarily, and through becoming servants of God, in male hands. Yet the symbolization of God as a patriarchal male and Israel as wife, son, and servant of God creates a basic analogy of woman and nature. God is the ultimate patriarchal Lord, under whom the human patriarchal lord rules over women, children, slaves, and land.

The image of God as single, male, and transcendent, prior to nature, also shifts the symbolic relation of male consciousness to material life. Marduk was a young male god who was produced out of a process of theogony and cosmogony. He conquers and shapes the cosmos out of the body of an older Goddess that existed prior to himself, within which he himself stands. The Hebrew God exists above and prior to the cosmos, shaping it out of a chaos that is under his control. Genesis 2 gives us a parallel view of the male, not as the child of woman, but as the source of woman. She arises out of him, with the help of the male God, and is handed over to him as her Master.

The Greek World

When we turn to Greek philosophical myth, the link between mother and matter is made explicit. Plato, in his creation myth, the *Timaeus,* speaks of primal, unformed matter as the receptacle and "nurse." He imagines a disembodied male mind as divine architect, or Demiurgos, shaping this matter into the cosmos by fashioning it after the intellectual blueprint of the Eternal Ideas. These Eternal Ideas exist in an immaterial, transcendent world of Mind, separate from and above the material stuff that he is fashioning into the visible cosmos.

The World Soul is also created by the Demiurgos, by mixing together dynamics of antithetical relations (the Same and the Other). This world soul is infused into the body of the cosmos in order to make it move in harmonic motion. The remnants of this world soul are divided into bits, to create the souls of humans. These souls are first placed in the stars, so that human souls will gain knowledge of the Eternal Ideas. Then the souls are sown in the bodies of humans on earth. The task of the soul is to govern the unruly passions that arise from the body.

If the soul succeeds in this task, it will return at death to its native star and there live a life of leisured contemplation. If not, the soul will be reincarnated into the body of a woman or an animal, and it will then have to work its way back into the form of an (elite) male and finally escape from bodily reincarnation altogether, to return to its original disincarnate form in the starry realm above. Plato takes for granted an ontological hierarchy of being, the immaterial intellectual world over material cosmos, and, within this ontological hierarchy, the descending hierarchy of male, female, and animal.

In the Greco-Roman era, a sense of pessimism about the possibility of blessing and well-being within the bodily, historical world deepened in Eastern Mediterranean culture, expressing itself in apocalypticism and gnosticism. In apocalypticism, God is seen as intervening in history to destroy the present sinful and finite world of human society and nature and to create a new heaven and earth freed from both sin and death. In gnosticism, mystical philosophies chart the path to salvation by way of withdrawal of the soul from the body and its passions and its return to an immaterial realm outside of and above the visible cosmos.

Christianity

Early Christianity was shaped by both the Hebraic and Greek traditions, including their alienated forms in apocalypticism and gnosticism. Second-century Christianity struggled against gnosticism, reaffirming the Hebraic view of nature and body as God's good creation. The second-century Christian theologian Irenaeus sought to combat gnostic anticosmism and to synthesize apocalypticism and Hebraic creationalism. He imaged the whole cosmos as a bodying forth of the Word and Spirit of God, as the sacramental embodiment of the invisible God.

Sin arises through a human denial of this relation to God. But salvific grace, dispensed progressively through the Hebrew and Christian revelations, allows humanity to heal its relation to God. The cosmos, in turn, grows into being a blessed and immortalized manifestation of the divine Word and Spirit, which is its ground of being.

However, Greek and Latin Christianity, increasingly influenced by Neoplatonism, found this materialism distasteful. They deeply imbibed the platonic eschatology of the escape of the soul from the body and its return to a transcendent world outside the earth. The earth and the body must be left behind in order to ascend to another, heavenly world of disembodied life. Even though the Hebrew idea of resurrection of the body was retained, increasingly this notion was envisioned as a vehicle of immortal light for the soul, not the material body, in all its distasteful physical processes, which they saw as the very essence of sin as mortal corruptibility.

The view of women in this ascetic Christian system was profoundly ambivalent. A part of ascetic Christianity imagined women becoming freed from subordination, freed both for equality in salvation and to act as agents of Christian preaching and teaching. But this freedom was based on woman rejecting her sexuality and reproductive role and becoming symbolically male. The classic Christian "good news" to woman as equal to man in Christ was rooted in a misogynist view of female sexuality and reproduction as the essence of the sinful, mortal, corruptible life.

For most male ascetic Christians, even an ascetic woman, who had rejected her sexuality and reproductive role, was too dangerously sexual. Ascetic women were increasingly deprived of their minor roles in public ministry, such as deaconess, and locked away in convents, where obedience to God was to be expressed in total obedience to male ecclesiastical authority. Sexual woman, drawing male seminal power into herself, her womb swelling with new life, became the very essence of sin, corruptibility, and death, from which the male ascetic fled. Eternal life was disembodied male soul, freed from all material underpinnings in the mortal bodily life, represented by woman and nature.

Medieval Latin Christianity was also deeply ambivalent about its view of nature. One side of medieval thought retained something of Irenaeus's sacramental cosmos, which becomes the icon of God through feeding on the redemptive power of Christ in the sacraments of bread and wine. The redeemed cosmos as resurrected body, united with God, is possible only by freeing the body of its sexuality and mortality. Mary, the virgin Mother of Christ, assumed into heaven to reign by the side of her son, was the representative of this redeemed body of the cosmos, the resurrected body of the Church.

But the dark side of Medieval thought saw nature as possessed by demonic powers that draw us down to sin and death through sexual temptation. Women, particularly old crones with sagging breasts and bellies, still perversely retaining their sexual appetites, are the vehicles of the demonic power of nature. They are the witches who sell their souls to the Devil in a satanic parody of the Christian sacraments.

The Reformation and the Scientific Revolution

The Calvinist Reformation and the Scientific Revolution in England in the late sixteenth and seventeenth centuries represent key turning points in the Western concept of nature. In these two movements, the Medieval struggle between the sacramental and the demonic views of nature was recast. Calvinism dismembered the Medieval sacramental sense of nature. For Calvinism, nature was totally depraved. There was no residue of divine presence in it that could sustain a natural knowledge or relation to God. Saving knowledge of God descends from on high, beyond nature, in the revealed World available only in Scripture, as preached by the Reformers.

The Calvinist reformers were notable in their iconoclastic hostility toward visual art. Stained glass, statues, and carvings were smashed, and the churches stripped of all visible imagery. Only the disembodied Word, descending from the preacher to the ear of the listener, together with music, could be bearers of divine presence. Nothing one could see, touch, taste, or smell was trustworthy as bearer of the divine. Even the bread and wine were no longer the physical embodiment of Christ, but intellectual reminders of the message about Christ's salvific act enacted in the past.

Calvinism dismantled the sacramental world of Medieval Christianity, but it maintained and reinforced its demonic universe. The fallen world, especially physical nature and other human groups outside of the control of the Calvinist church, lay in the grip of the Devil. All who were labeled pagan, whether Catholics or Indians and Africans, were the playground of demonic powers. But, even within the Calvinist church, women were the gateway of the Devil. If women were completely obedient to their fathers, husbands, ministers, and magistrates, they might be redeemed as goodwives. But in any independence of women lurked heresy and witchcraft. Among Protestants, Calvinists were the primary witch-hunters.

The Scientific Revolution at first moved in a different direction, exorcizing the demonic powers from nature in order to reclaim it as an icon of divine reason manifest in natural law. But, in the seventeenth and eighteenth centuries, the more animist natural science, which unified material and spiritual, lost out to a strict dualism of transcendent intellect and dead matter. Nature was secularized. It was no longer the scene of a struggle between Christ and the Devil. Both divine and demonic spirits were driven out of it. In Cartesian dualism and Newtonian physics, it becomes matter in motion, dead stuff moving obediently, according to mathematical laws knowable to a new male elite of scientists. With no life or soul of its own, nature could be safely expropriated by this male elite and infinitely reconstructed to augment its wealth and power.

In Western society, the application of science to technological control over nature marched side by side with colonialism. From the sixteenth to the twentieth centuries, Western Europeans would appropriate the lands of the Americas, Asia, and Africa, and reduce their human populations to servitude. The wealth accrued by this vast expropriation of land and labor would fuel new levels of technological revolution, transforming material resources into new forms of energy and mechanical work, control of disease, and increasing speed of communication and travel. Western elites grew increasingly optimistic, imagining that this technological way of life would gradually conquer all problems of material scarcity and even push back the limits of human mortality. The Christian dream of immortal blessedness, freed from finite limits, was translated into scientific technological terms.

Ecological Crisis

. . . This Western scientific Industrial Revolution has been built on injustice. It has been based on the takeover of the land, its agricultural, metallic, and mineral wealth appropriated through the exploitation of the labor of the indigenous people. This wealth has flowed back to enrich the West, with some for local elites, while the laboring people of these lands grew poorer. This system of global affluence, based on exploitation of the land and labor of the many for the benefit of the few, with its high consumption of energy and waste, cannot be expanded to include the poor without destroying the basis of life of the planet itself. We are literally destroying the air, water, and soil upon which human and planetary life depend.

In order to preserve the unjust monopoly on material resources from the growing protests of the poor, the world became more and more militarized. Most nations have been using the lion's share of their state budgets for weapons, both to guard against one another and to control their own poor. Weapons also become one of the major exports of wealthy nations to poor nations. Poor nations grow increasingly indebted to wealthy nations while buying weapons to repress their own impoverished masses. Population explosion, exhaustion of natural resources, pollution, and state violence are the four horsemen of the new global apocalypse.

The critical question of both justice and survival is how to pull back this disastrous course and remake our relations with one another and with the earth.

Toward an Ecofeminist Ethic and Culture

There are many elements that need to go into an ecofeminist ethic and culture for a just and sustainable planet. One element is to reshape our dualistic concept of reality as split between soulless matter and transcendent male consciousness. We need to discover our actual reality as latecomers to the planet. The world of nature, plants, and animals existed billions of years before we came on the scene. Nature does not need us to rule over it, but runs itself very well, even better, without humans. We are the parasites on the food chain of life, consuming more and more, and putting too little back to restore and maintain the life system that supports us.

We need to recognize our utter dependence on the great life-producing matrix of the planet in order to learn to reintegrate our human systems of production, consumption, and waste into the ecological patterns by which nature sustains life. This might begin by revisualizing the relation of mind, or human intelligence, to nature. Mind or consciousness is not something that originates in some transcendent world outside of nature, but is the place where nature itself becomes conscious. We need to think of human consciousness not as separating us as a higher species from the rest of nature, but rather as a gift to enable us to learn how to harmonize our needs with the natural system around us, of which we are a dependent part.

Such a reintegration of human consciousness and nature must reshape the concept of God, instead of modeling God after alienated male consciousness, outside of and ruling over nature. God, in ecofeminist spirituality, is the immanent source of life that sustains the whole planetary community. God is neither male nor anthropomorphic. God is the font from which the variety of plants and animals well up in each new generation, the matrix that sustains their life-giving interdependency with one another.

In ecofeminist culture and ethic, mutual interdependency replaces the hierarchies of domination as the model of relationship between men and women, between human groups and between humans and other beings. All racist, sexist, classist, cultural, and anthropocentric assumptions of the superiority of whites over blacks, males over females, managers over workers, humans over animals and plants, must be discarded. In a real sense, the so-called superior pole in each relation is actually the more dependent side of the relationship.

But it is not enough simply to humbly acknowledge dependency. The pattern of male-female, racial, and class interdependency itself has to be reconstructed socially, creating more equitable sharing in the work and the fruits of work, rather than making one side of the relation the subjugated and impoverished base for the power and wealth of the other.

In terms of male-female relations, this means not simply allowing women more access to public culture, but converting males to an equal share in the tasks of child nurture and household maintenance. A revolution in female roles into the male work world, without a corresponding revolution in male roles, leaves the basic pattern of patriarchal exploitation of women untouched. Women are simply overworked in a new way, expected to do both a male workday, at low pay, and also the unpaid work of women that sustains family life.

There must be a conversion of men to the work of women, along with the conversion of male consciousness to the earth. Such conversions will reshape the symbolic vision of salvation.

Instead of salvation sought either in the disembodied soul or the immortalized body, in a flight to heaven or to the end of history, salvation should be seen as continual conversion to the center, to the concrete basis by which we sustain our relation to nature and to one another. In every day and every new generation, we need to remake our relation with one another, finding anew the true nexus of relationality that sustains, rather than exploits and destroys, life.

Finally, ecofeminist culture must reshape our basic sense of self in relation to the life cycle. The sustaining of an organic community of plant and animal life is a continual cycle of growth and disintegration. The Western flight from mortality is a flight from the disintegration side of the life cycle, from accepting ourselves as part of that process. By pretending that we can immortalize ourselves, souls and bodies, we are immortalizing our garbage and polluting the earth. In order to learn to recycle our garbage as fertilizer for new life, as matter for new artifacts, we need to accept our selfhood as participating in the same process. Humans also are finite organisms, centers of experience in a life cycle that must disintegrate back into the nexus of life and arise again in new forms.

These conversions, from alienated, hierarchical dualism to life-sustaining mutuality, will radically change the patterns of patriarchal culture. Basic concepts, such as God, soul-body, and salvation will be reconceived in ways that may bring us much closer to the ethical values of love, justice, and care for the earth. These values have been proclaimed by patriarchal religion, yet contradicted by patriarchal symbolic and social patterns of relationship.

These tentative explorations of symbolic changes must be matched by a new social practice that can incarnate these conversions in new social and technological ways of organizing human life in relation to one another and to nature. This will require a new sense of urgency about the untenability of present patterns of life and compassionate solidarity with those who are its victims.

Questions for Reflection on Rosemary Radford Ruether

1 Ruether appears to assume that if one believes in human immortality (either as disembodied souls or in "immortalized" bodies), then one will adopt an exploitative attitude toward nature. Is there a necessary connection between these? Might a person believe in human immortality and also have respect, even reverence, for God's creation? Or might one reject the idea that humans have a dimension that transcends nature and nonetheless adopt a greedy and exploitative attitude toward nature?
2. Do you think Ruether is right that culturally women have been associated with the body and nature? Is there not also a tradition of thinking that associates women with our higher and

more spiritual aspirations? Consider, for example, Dante's Beatrice, or the view of femininity expressed so powerfully in Goethe's *Faust*: "Eternal womanhood leads us above." Would Ruether disapprove of those female saints and mystics who have passionately desired eternal life with God above all else? Should she?

3. Is it possible to create a society in which all hierarchies are abolished? What about the authority of adults over children?

4. Is Ruether's own vision an egalitarian one? Would it be possible to institute the sort of radical social changes she advocates by consensus, or would some sort of political hierarchy be necessary in order to mandate and enforce the necessary policies? Consider, also, whether her ideal society would require more behavioral changes of men than of women. Will women go on doing what they are doing, or be free to choose? If they are free to choose but men are not, how would Ruether respond to the charge that this is unfair?

5. What implications would Ruether's "ecofeminist ethic and culture" have for the question of abortion and why?

Women in Genesis 1–3

EDITH BLACK

Edith Black provides a commentary on the first three chapters of Genesis. Patriarchy, she maintains, was not part of God's original plan, but this does not mean that God's creation contains no gender-specific roles. The representative role of Adam provides the most adequate explanation for why God limited the Hebrew priesthood to selected males. The name given to Eve stresses her role as originator and preserver of life. While females as well as males can represent God before man as prophets, the prophetic vocation cannot be transmitted through institutional channels as can the priestly office.

The first three chapters of Genesis constitute, in Judeo-Christian eyes, an inspired origin story, which recounts the foundational creative events that establish the ecological-social order intended by the creator and its subsequent distortion.

In Genesis the creation of man and woman represents the climax of a series of creative events that proceed from what we would call the material universe, "heaven and earth," to plants and sentient animals. The uniqueness of humans, however, is apparent from the fact that they are created in the image of God, which is understood in the rest of Scripture to mean that they have the capacity to reason on the basis of moral law. This is not to be confused with the capacity to think, which the higher sentient animals have to some degree or another. Because of their rational capacity, men and women have a vocation to cooperatively govern the rest of creation and, in so doing, both equally manifest the creator's own image in creation:

Written for this volume. Published with the author's permission.

Let us make man in our own image, after our likeness; and let them have dominion over the fish of the sea, and over the birds of the air, and over the cattle, and over all the earth, and over every creeping thing that creeps upon the earth.

The affinity of human beings with the rest of the created natural order is apparent from the first commands God gives to them in Genesis 1: to "be fruitful and multiply." This command reiterates the command already given to sentient animals—those beings that have "nephesh," translated as "soul" or "life."

The second command, "to fill the earth and subdue it; to have dominion over the fish of the sea and over the birds of the air and over every living thing that moves upon the earth," bestows on man the right to rule. But rule here means the same as it does elsewhere in the Old Testament—a just distribution of resources that considers the needs of the ruled as much as those of the rulers. In the Old Testament, rightful rule always means stewardship, not subjugation.

At the end of Genesis 1, all living beings having "nephesh" are allocated plants as their means of subsistence, so humans in their role of managing creation are not to allocate all resources for themselves so other creatures cannot survive. Furthermore, Genesis 2 makes it clear that dominion does not mean antagonistic relationships between man and the rest of creation. Adam, the first man, is put into a garden and told to "till and keep" it. The animals all come to him, unafraid, to be named. Both Genesis 1 and 2 therefore seem to suggest that predation between animals and between man and animals is not part of God's original intent for creation.

It was not until the Fall, described in Genesis 3, and developed further in the history of the flood in Genesis 9, that the ecological and social disintegration of the original creative order occurs as the result of human misuse of their capacity to reason—their attempt to become like a god, "knowing good and evil"—in other words, to set themselves up as the arbiters of moral right and wrong, rather than rely upon God. The fruitful garden that humans tilled becomes an unyielding ground from which they must wrest a living: "cursed is the ground because of you; and in toil you shall eat of it all the days of your life." And after the flood the companionship between man and animals that God had intended breaks down into a relationship of hunter and hunted:

The fear of you and the dread of you shall be upon every beast of the earth, and upon every bird of the air, upon everything that creeps on the ground, and all the fish of the sea; into your hand they are delivered. Every moving thing that lives shall be food for you; as I gave you the green plants, I give you everything.

Only after the Fall does the copartnership of man and woman in stewarding the earth degenerate into the patriarchal order that feminists decry: "your desire shall be for your husband and he shall rule over you."

It is clear from the ordering of creation events in both Genesis 1 and 2 that at each successive stage creatures come into being which are of greater value than those created previously. Therefore, any interpretation of the creation of Eve after the creation of Adam as implying secondary status has no validity. In fact, the Hebrew word "helpmeet" incorporates a Hebrew word "helper" that is usually used of Yahweh, therefore meaning "helper" from a position of strength.

Moreover, the fact that Eve leads Adam astray should not be taken to imply that she is less rational than he is. For her decision to take the fruit is not primarily an act of sensual desire but one of inordinate spiritual ambition to become like a god.

Thus the patriarchal order was not part of God's original order. This does not mean, however, that there is no gender-based role distinction intrinsic to God's creation. Indeed, Genesis 1:26–27 stresses the fact that God created man in the image of himself as male and female: "So God created man in his own image, in the image of God he created him; male and female he created them." In other words, humanity always manifests itself sexually as male or female—never as neuter.

Genesis 1:26–27 thus seems to point to a fundamental role distinction rooted in the created order that every culture, patriarchal or otherwise, prior to our modern technological one, has recognized. Anthropological evidence indicates that men universally take on the higher-risk roles such as defense, while women everywhere take on the more nurturing roles such as caring for small children—though, admittedly, many of the tasks assigned to each sex have been culturally imposed and are not intrinsic to the basic role distinction between male and female.

The second account of the creation of man, Genesis 2:7, 21–22, gives us a clue to what the basic distinction is in the names bestowed upon our original parents. The first human being is a male whose name "Adam" constitutes the generic name for mankind. The role unique to males thus seems to be a representative one. The male embodies in himself the unity of the group which he represents—both in the order of nature, as with Adam who embodied in himself the unity of all humanity, and in the order of grace, as with Christ who embodies in himself the unity of the new humanity.

I believe the representative role of males provides the most adequate explanation for why God limited Hebrew priesthood to selected males—those descended from Aaron—and allowed only male animals without blemish to serve as sacrificial victims, in contrast to the general practice in the Ancient Near East, which permitted priestesses. The representative role of both priests and sacrificial victims was especially apparent once a year when the high priest stood before God in the Holy of Holies in the stead of his people to make an offering for the atonement of their sins. The priest transferred their sins into one of the victims, a male goat, by laying his hands upon its head, and then drove it into the desert.[1]

Both the high priest, who offered in Israel's stead, and the unblemished male victim, who stood in Israel's stead for her sins, are types of Christ. They prefigure the ultimate high priest who serves at the altar in heaven and the ultimate sacrificial victim on the cross whose blood was sprinkled on that altar.[2] It was because Christ's primary role on earth was to serve as the lamb of God who took our sins upon himself that he was born a male. It was because his primary role in Heaven is to serve as the high priest who mediates between us and the Father that he rose again in a glorified male body.

The name of the second human being created by God, Eve, likewise gives us a clue to the unique female role. Her name, which means both "she who causes to live" and "she who keeps alive," stresses woman's role as originator and preserver of life. Adam honors her life-creating role further by calling her "the mother of all living"—an epithet which parallels that borne by Ancient Near Eastern mother goddesses, "mother of all the gods."[3]

When Eve gives birth to her first child she names him Cain from a Hebrew verb meaning "to create" and says: "I have created a man with Yahweh." She thus emphasizes the unique partnership between a woman and God in bringing forth human life. For it is with her body that God repeats the miracle of creation by infusing a soul into the material embryo provided by herself and her husband. The Old Testament repeatedly stresses Yahweh's intimate involvement in procreation from conception to birth. He opens and closes the womb to male sperm[4] and fashions the unborn child.[5]

Many secular feminists claim that any emphasis on the unique capacity of women to create new human life constitutes a "biology is destiny" type of argument. Yet in so doing they accept the very biological reductionism they decry, for they overlook the fact that, as all religions testify, sexual intercourse among human beings is a spiritual as well as a biological act—manifesting a mystical unity as well as fulfilling a biological urge. Genesis 2:14–28 figuratively represents this unity by the formation of Eve from Adam's rib and by his recognition of her as "bone of my bone and flesh of my flesh." They become "one flesh," a living organism in itself. In Ephesians 25:31–32 the matrimonial union of husband and wife reflects the mystical union between Christ and his church:

> For this reason a man shall leave his father and mother and be joined to his wife, and the two shall become one. This is the great mystery and I take it to mean Christ and the Church.

Therefore, human sexuality, while incorporating the bodily sexuality of animals, also transcends it.

Old Testament prophets decried the worship of human procreative powers in the form of Canaanite male and female deities. But they never desacralized human sexuality, reducing it to a merely biological phenomenon, as does our modern secular culture. The Old Testament upholds the sacredness of the procreative process without falling into the pagan error of deifying it.

Scripture further indicates that the differentiation of man (Adam) into male and female reflects a differentiation within God himself. Surely it is not accidental that, when God is portrayed as deliberating with himself in contemplation of the creation of man as male and female, he refers to himself as plural: "Let us make man in our image. . . ." Whatever human explanation scholars may offer for the author's choice of the plural in this passage—the royal we or the plural of majesty—the fact remains that God inspired that choice with some purpose in mind.[6]

I think the personalized wisdom figure of Proverbs, the Wisdom of Solomon, Sirach, and Baruch, whom early Christians identified with the pre-existent Christ—an identification which St. Paul also seems to make in I Corinthians 1:21–24—indicates that the male and female roles that God incorporates in himself are the male representational and female creative roles. For it cannot be accidental that the creative intelligence of Yahweh is hypothesized in the Old Testament as "Wisdom," a word of female gender, and not as "Word," a word of the masculine gender. The word of God never develops into a personal figure in the Old Testament as it does in the New,[7] even though its function as an agent of creation in Genesis and as an effector of historical events in the prophetic writings would have allowed such a development.

It would seem that the Old Testament writers hypothesized the creative intelligence of Yahweh as a female figure because the focus of their interest is on her role as a cocreator and preserver of the created order.[8] Wisdom is a motherly figure who bears within herself the model ideas from which each created being takes its form and the model laws to which each created being conforms its behavior. She invokes men as her "sons" to conform their ways to hers because they alone of all earthly creatures have the intelligence and freedom to choose to do otherwise.

The New Testament writers, on the other hand, use predominantly male imagery to describe the word made flesh (the second person of the Trinity) even in his pre-existent role as the agent of creation, because the focus of their interest is on his incarnational role as the representative man who embodies in himself all humanity and through all humanity the created order.[9]

It would seem also that the fact that Christ, the second person of the Trinity, is the source of truth—whether expressed in the feminine intuitive mode (Wisdom) or in the masculine logical mode (Word)—lies at the basis of the fact that females as well as males function as his prophetic spokespeople. The Old Testament provides a number of examples of women serving as prophetesses: Miriam, Moses's sister; Deborah, one of the early Hebrew judges; Huldah, in the reign of Josiah; and Isaiah's wife. Acts in the New Testament also portrays several women acting as prophetesses in the early church.

Prophets, female as well as male, played as crucial a role in the formation of the Yahweh faith as those who held cultic office. For example, Miriam led Israel out of Egypt along with

Moses and Aaron; Deborah inspired her people to fight Yahweh's battles against the oppressing Canaanites; and Huldah authorized one of the most important Yahwist reform movements in Israel's history, acting as King Josiah's prophetic counselor.

Females as well as males, therefore, represent God before man as his prophets, though only males represent men before God as his priests. The prophetic vocation cannot be transmitted through institutional channels, as can be priestly office. For the prophet or prophetess delivers a direct communication from God applicable to a specific historical circumstance, while the priest in his role as teacher explicates the law of God applicable to all times.[10]

The ultimate consummation of Eve's role as "mother of all living" is implicit in Genesis 3 when God addresses the tempter Satan, represented by the serpent: "I will put enmity between you and the woman, and between your seed and her seed; he shall bruise your head and you shall bruise his heel."

For it is through Mary, seen by the early church as the "new Eve," that the effects of the Fall are overcome. In giving birth to Christ, the "new Adam," she becomes the mother of God and, as such, a "mother" to all reborn in Christ, her son. Her free assent to God's will provides for us a model of humanity created in the image of God.

Notes

1. Leviticus 15:1–34.
2. Hebrews 5:10–15.
3. Isaac Kikawada, "Two Notes on Eve," *Journal of Biblical Literature* 91 (1972), 33–37.
4. A good example is the story of childless Hannah in I Samuel 1:5–6, 19–20. See also Genesis *passim*.
5. Psalm 139:13–16; Job 10:8–11; Isaiah 45:9–18, 49:2; Jeremiah 1:5.
6. For Christians, the fuller sense of this use of the royal we or plural of majesty becomes clear in light of Christ's revelation that God exists in three persons.
7. See especially John 1:1–3.
8. Job 28:12–27; Proverbs 3:19–20, 8:22–31; Wisdom of Solomon 7:22–8:1, 9:1–4; Sirach 15:2.
9. Romans 8:19–25; Ephesians 1:9–10.
10. Deuteronomy 31:9–12.

Questions for Reflection on Edith Black

1. Are you persuaded by Black's interpretation of Genesis 1–3? How is her account different from Ruether's, and which do you find more persuasive? Could they both be right?
2. If patriarchy is not part of God's original plan, does this mean that we can get rid of it? Many contemporary Christians believe strongly in the headship and authority of fathers within their families. Might they argue that in a fallen world such authority is necessary even if it was not God's original intention?
3. How does Black's argument apply to leadership positions in the church? Are religious leaders significantly different from political leaders with respect to her argument? Are Catholic priests different from Protestant ministers?
4. Explain the meaning and symbolism of the names given to Adam and Eve. What conclusions does Black draw from these? Do they represent unfortunate sex stereotypes, or do they express a deep truth about men and women?
5. Compare and contrast Black with Frankiel (see next article) on the appropriate role of women and the feminine element in religious life.

Traditional Judaism and Feminine Spirituality

TAMAR FRANKIEL

Tamar Frankiel attempts to introduce a woman's voice into the Jewish tradition. God, she argues, need not be understood as "uniquely alone": rather, God's oneness, the divine unity, is a marriage of male and female, the transcendent unity which is neither mind nor body, spirit nor matter, nor anything else we can understand.

Women in the twentieth century are "finding their voices." This is perhaps the great theme of modern women's lives: we who have been silent are speaking out, describing ourselves, our experiences, our points of view in our own ways rather than—as in the past—having no voice at all or having our ideas filtered through the speech and writings of men. In religious thought—and here we will be referring to modern Christian and Jewish thought unless otherwise noted—this has resulted in a dramatic awakening and the development of ideas that sometimes seem to have the potential of reconstructing our ways of thinking altogether. . . .

We cannot consider the whole range of feminist thought here. We will be able to touch on only a few areas that in my opinion are the most crucial for Jewish women's self-understanding and self-esteem. One of the things we want to know is whether—even if we love Jewish tradition and practice—we are buying into a system that undercuts our full humanity, our full womanhood. Many Jewish feminists believe that we (along with women in most other religious traditions) cannot participate with integrity in our tradition unless we make radical changes. Although . . . there are many elements in our tradition that are richly relevant to women and positive for our growth, they could argue that we are fooling ourselves. Perhaps these are

Tamar Frankiel from *The Voice of Sarah: Feminine Spirituality and Traditional Judaism.* Harper Collins, 1990. Used with permission of publisher.

marginal features, while the core of tradition remains misogynist and oppressive to women. This issue needs to be addressed directly.

The way I have chosen to approach the question is to examine some of the leading writings in feminist religious thought. Many feminists are finding fundamental currents in women's spirituality that seem to appear cross-culturally and that have been opposed, denigrated, or forced underground by male dominance in religion. They have also found persistent habits of thought—basic philosophical assumptions about the nature of things—that are negative toward women and our kinds of spirituality. We must examine the extent to which these negative elements are present in Judaism and whether Jewish tradition allows and encourages women's self-expression in positive, significant ways.

To begin with fundamentals: one of the most important and recurrent issues discussed in feminist literature is the dualistic framework of Western religious thought that associates the feminine with negative characteristics. Most Western philosophical and religious thinkers assume a division between spirit and matter, or mind and body, such that spirit and mind are superior to matter and body. Further, the male is associated with spirit, the female with matter. This is worked out in a series of correlated oppositions reflected in many varieties of religious thought. Here is a partial list:

spirit/matter
mind/body
transcendence/immanence
supernatural/natural
intellect/senses
God/human beings
reason/emotion
male/female

In almost every case the first of the two is presented as superior, the second as inferior.

A second major issue has to do with the standards set for development along the spiritual path. . . . The lone ascetic in his cell, the prophet on a mountaintop, and the charismatic leader of a religious organization all emphasize the singular individual and achieving a place at the top of a hierarchy. Feminists suggest that while we may value our private communion with God, women's spirituality is essentially relational, as is expressed in one of the movement's favorite images: weaving webs of relations between self and other selves, self and world. How the experience of the individual interfaces with the networks of others is one of the cutting edges of feminist thought. But it is clear that a strongly relational orientation prevails, giving feminine spirituality a definite communal and moral/ethical bent from the beginning.

A third, related issue is the role of emotion in self and mind. Feminists tend to reject pure intellectual analysis for a more engaged, involved, or personal style. This brings us back again to the oppositions that are inherent in much of Western thought: mind and reason are usually pitted against emotion and sensuality, with reason being taken as the ultimate arbiter in human affairs. Feminists argue that cutting ourselves off from emotion and feeling has created forms of spirituality that are inadequate, unsatisfying, and ultimately unethical.

These problems are, as we will see, interrelated, but let us take them one by one before we weave them together. First, the feminist struggle with the inherited dualistic categories of Western thought—the oppositions cited above—goes back at least to Simone de Beauvoir's *The Second Sex* (1949), in which she developed an existentialist critique of Western culture's oppression of women. She showed how woman and the feminine are habitually regarded as being on the side of nature, the body, the irrational, and, theologically, "immanence." She insisted that women must refuse to accept these male definitions and regard themselves instead as "transcendent subjects"—creative and not merely receptive, initiating and not treated as an object, the Other. This means that we must affirm our freedom as creative individuals, using that liberty to move "outward, forward, and upward." . . .

Recently, however, another view has emerged. Here works like Susan Griffin's *Woman and Nature* (1978) have been extremely powerful. Griffin and others affirm that the feminine is indeed deeply connected with "nature" and "immanence," as de Beauvoir held, but this is not negative: embodiment is part of our deeply feminine mode of being. Creativity emerges from our bodies, from our physical nature, and our finite limitations, not in negation of them. We must affirm these deeply natural parts of ourselves and at the same time undercut the negative force of the dualistic system. Rosemary Radford Ruether, who sees the "dualism of nature and transcendence, matter and spirit as female against male" as "basic to male theology" insists that both sides must be rejected: "mother-matter-matrix as 'static immanence'" and "spirit and transcendence as rootless, antinatural, originating in an 'other world' beyond the cosmos."

The feminist revaluation of immanence is most clearly articulated in writings concerning women's intuited connection with the world, our sense of being inseparably a part of nature and the universe. Many have found compelling Alice Walker's characterization of women's spirituality in *The Color Purple,* when her character Shug describes herself as having "that feeling of being part of everything, not separate at all. I knew that if I cut a tree, my arm would bleed." . . .

We can see here how the feminist emphasis on immanence, undercutting what women have experienced as an oppressive dualism, connects with two other aspects of women's thought:

relatedness, that is, an inner sense of connection, and reliance on feeling as a ground for judgment and knowledge. If the universe is conceived of as simply the arena of fixed natural law, or as nature wild and untamed, it gives us no ground for moral judgments—one needs a transcendent lawmaker who provides laws for both nature and human beings and some mode, beyond nature, of implanting morality in the human being. But in Carol Christ's view, it is relatedness, love and caring, and a felt connection with other beings that provide, within our human nature, reasons for acting morally. This felt relationship is fundamental to women's spirituality. As she and Judith Plaskow write, the feminist sense of the self "is essentially relational, inseparable from the limiting and enriching contexts of body, feeling, relationship, community, history, and the web of life. The notion of the relational self can be correlated with the immanent turn in feminist views of the sacred: in both cases connection to that which is finite, changing, and limited is affirmed." Over against the philosopher Descartes, whose famous "I think, therefore I am" described the rational, disembodied, solitary ego, the feminine self is embodied, passionate, relational, communal. From this point of view, religious thinkers who talk about God as "being itself" or the "wholly other"—or in Judaism those who translate *Adonai echad* as "God is uniquely alone"—imply that God's lack of relatedness is a source of strength. For feminists only that divinity which is deeply related in and to the world can be authentic. . . . For these writers, relationships, connection to nature, and immanence all intertwine in their understanding of feminine spirituality.

Such features are not at all alien to what our tradition has handed down about Jewish women and the feminine. . . . In our discussion of ritual, we saw that woman's connection to nature is a persistent element. Feminine heroines and themes are strongly associated with the seasonal cycles; and women are associated with the moon, with motherhood, with food and nurturing, and with nature's sexual cycles. Whether in holidays like Rash Chodesh or special mitzvot like challah and niddah, women bring a spiritual dimension to the practical, real-life, finite embodiment of human beings.

Jewish women's life also emphasizes relationships and relatedness, with a strong connection to the concrete and personal aspects of life and a sense of interdependence. Women's traditional affinity for Tehillim (Psalms) suggests an appreciation both for nature and for personal, related spirituality—King David's intimate relation with God through all his various hardships and victories had great appeal. The women of our stories too were deeply concerned with relationships—first with family, particularly with husbands and children, then with the larger destiny of their descendants and the Jewish people as a whole.

We observed also that the very idea of motherhood in this tradition carries a strong sense of responsibility for the future: the women knew their actions would shape destiny. Jewish women were not trapped in "static immanence." On the contrary, the woman "looks smilingly to the future" and exerts her power to shape it. We saw that women often took risks and did the unconventional. Indeed, the stories of Jewish women suggest the truth of the description of premodern women given by Beverly Harrison when she says, "Historically, I believe, women have always exemplified the power of activity over passivity, of experimentation over routinization, of creativity and risk-taking over conventionality."

Jewish women are portrayed as oriented toward the immanent, the practical, and the web of relations for which they have considerable responsibility. Yet we are not simply immersed in material concerns. Jewish tradition sees us as essentially inward beings, whose essence revolves around the private sphere. The saying "All the glory of the daughter of the king is on the inside" focuses on that inwardness. That woman is the ruler of Shabbat, the day of inward orientation—toward home, community, and personal spirituality—exemplifies this also. On a personal level Channah as the model for prayer is an example: a woman deeply connected to her feelings expressing herself to God. In the prophetic consciousness of Sarah, Rivkah, and others we also see a strong inwardness: women had their own base of knowledge that came from within. Tamar, Yehudit, and Esther all acted outside the boundaries of what was usually considered proper and right on the basis of their inner moral certainty. Thus Judaism has recognized the inner strength of women and extolled it as a feminine virtue. This actually deepens what feminists have said about basing our knowledge and morality on our inner sense of things, including our feelings and intuitions. Jewish tradition suggests that, beyond feelings and emotions, feminine consciousness can operate at a level that approaches the prophetic....

... Some feminists have claimed that while there may be feminine dimensions to Jewish religious life, they are not really valued in Judaism—synagogue, yeshiva, and law court are more important. From an experiential point of view, many women and men within traditional Judaism will affirm that this is simply not so. Torah life is a total way of life, with women's responsibilities just as serious as men's, and equally highly valued. The question perhaps is whether women have appreciated the importance of affirming this dimension of their lives and speaking publicly about it. In the past most of the life of women remained private. In modern times, as traditional communities disintegrated, Jewish women's occupations—as with other women—were denigrated and in addition were subject to the general Enlightenment criticism of obsolete ritual. It is only in recent times that women involved in traditional practice have begun to break the silence about their experience.

Even if we grant the strengths of Jewish women in the past, there is still more to the feminist argument: Is it not true that underneath the positive features we find in Judaism a negative valuation of women or of the feminine principle? Do not the spirit/matter, soul/body, transcendent/immanent polarities appear in Jewish thought in ways detrimental to the feminine side? They do; but differently than in Greek or Christian thought. In Jewish mystical thought, for example, we often find man or the masculine associated with spirit, woman with body; then body is associated with the "animal," and this in turn with the temptations that turn a person away from God. While Judaism never castigated Chava (Eve) and all women in the way Christianity did for bringing on the first sin, still the literature is laced with associations of the feminine to our animal nature and thus to spiritual danger. At the same time, Judaism has affirmed more consistently than Christianity a positive attitude toward body, nature, and world. Male and female are always seen as interdependent, though the male—particularly male anatomy—is the mystical model of humanity. Moreover, women are regarded as more spiritual than men. But it is clear that Judaism has absorbed to some degree the dualistic presuppositions of Western—particularly Greek—thought that tend to devalue the feminine.

Another example: the two names of God most frequently used in the Bible, "Adonai" and "Elohim," are associated with the masculine and feminine, respectively. The first is connected to the aspect of God that expresses mercy, redemption, and the assertion of God's benign will acting from outside the universe as we know it. The second, feminine aspect is associated with nature, fixed law, the eternal round of things. The first is dynamic: God's action in history that makes possible new events, new revelations. The second, feminine, appears static, moving in eternal circles. In Judaism this second aspect of God expresses justice as well—the more severe side of God that, like nature, moves in terms of fixed laws of reward and punishment.

Let us look more closely at what is at stake here. First: can we have a more benign and intimate perception of God by eliminating the idea of transcendence with its masculine associations? It would seem not. From the traditional Jewish point of view, one cannot collapse the transcendence of God into the immanence of nature. The two dimensions are absolutely essential. If one had only a transcendent God, one would have an evil, or at best a neutral and mechanical, world. But if one had only an immanent God, taking the world of nature as divine, as feminists like Carol Christ wish to do, one would collapse into paganism. Nature has divinity within it, to be sure, but that is secondary, dependent on the transcendent Creator God who formed nature and gave it its fixed laws. God is immanent in the world, but that world is totally dependent for its existence on the continually acting transcendent will, the consciousness that lies beyond nature. (Translate: the feminine is entirely dependent for her creative power on the masculine.) Similarly, the transcendent God gave the Torah as the fixed system of laws for human beings. That same transcendent divine will which guides nature is the source of all guidelines for human action: the mitzvot and morality itself. His Torah given on Sinai is our guide, not any inner intuitions from the Shekhinah. (Translate: the masculine is the source of all morality.)

Yet part of the problem is our understanding of the word *transcendence*. Its common meaning is that which is above the limits of human thought—beyond good and evil, beyond mind and emotion, beyond male and female. In various usages, however, it takes on different connotations.

As we observed, in much of Western thought it has become attached to mind/spirit/reason as opposed to body/matter/emotion. But, in another context, the literary "transcendentalists" used the term to connote a kind of higher intuition, a Reason above ordinary rational logic. The term is itself subject to much confusion. We should take transcendence to mean that which precedes any levels of being or intelligence than we, in our human finitude, can know.

But we must understand this in a Jewish context. Our idea of transcendence derives from religious experiences different from those of the Greeks, who, from Plato on down, emphasized the split between spirit and matter. The primary experience that for Jewish tradition gave rise to the concept of transcendence, the name "Adonai," was the exodus from Egypt, God's redemption of the Jewish people. "Ask if any deed as mighty as this has been seen or heard!" exclaimed Moses. "Did ever a God attempt to come and take a nation for himself out of another nation, . . . as the Lord your God did for you in Egypt in the sight of all of you?" (Deut. 4.32–34). Rabbi Abraham Isaac Kook wrote that human "sovereignty over the world's lower creatures with an idealistic motivation"—that is, our moral sense of responsibility—"began to be manifested in the miracles and wonders of the exodus from Egypt, which stamped the Jewish people with its historic character." From the unfathomable work of God in redeeming a group of slaves first came the Jewish view that God transcends the world; for it was here, according to traditional thought, that God exceeded anything known in nature. God performed miracles to overturn nature and human rulership, to liberate the Israelite slaves.

Rosemary Ruether has pointed out many respects in which the Israelite God transcended "patriarchal consciousness." Calling Abraham away from his father's house, breaking the bonds between the overlord Pharaoh and his subjects signified that rules of father and son, master and slave, king and subject could be broken to establish a higher allegiance, an allegiance formed from love. Moreover, God did this in response to the "crying out" of the slaves. It was an act of mercy, not on the basis of merit. . . .

The point of view represented in Torah, prophets, and classical rabbinic interpretations holds that it is God's mercy—not his thought, mind, intellect, spirit, logos, or other Greek philosophical characteristics—that exemplifies his transcendence, because it comes from a place beyond the natural order of things. God, in Jewish thought from The Exodus down to modern times, is unimaginably loving, giving, compassionate, beneficent. As the great seventeenth-century thinker Moshe Chaim Luzzato taught, God's purpose in creation is to give of his goodness to his creatures.

But this is precisely what feminists demand of God: that s/he be related, compassionate, bountiful. Part of the natural feminine moral sensibility is to recognize bonds of love—between parent and child, man and woman, friend and friend, and even between strangers—which connect us all together. We see nature as interdependent and mutually supportive. We experience relations between people, as Carol Gilligan has pointed out, as matters of care, responsibility, and responsiveness, not primarily the balancing of claims according to rules of justice. These are all reflected in the way women experience God. And these same elements infuse the Jewish view of God: when we ask why God redeemed the Hebrew slaves, the Torah tells us that he heard their cries. It is an eminently feminine answer. One can argue that the Jewish people had merit—merit as Abraham's descendants, merit for maintaining their Jewish lives in the midst of Egyptian culture. But most simply, God heard their cries—like a mother whose child is crying, he could not let it go on any longer. So it is understandable that many women students ask me why "Adonai," the name of God representing mercy, should be male.

. . . Understood from a Jewish perspective, then, divine transcendence bridges across the supposedly male and female views. The one who redeems slaves, the one who carries the people to freedom as an eagle carries its young on its wings (Exod. 19:4; Deut. 32:11), the one who inspires Moses to care for them as a nursing father (!)—this divinity is intimately related to our lives. . . .

Yet we are not done with our Greek influences. We must look afresh at the concept of God that we have inherited from Genesis: that God is the Creator who makes the world *ex nihilo*, from nothing, and is totally independent of creation. Many feminists charge that this is another dimension of transcendence which emphasizes God's unrelatedness to us. They are attracted to myths of other cultures wherein a female deity creates the world from her own body or where the things of the world spring forth from a feminine earth. In contrast, Jewish tradition insists on the independence of the creator God who creates by his word. This later became connected with Greek concepts of transcendence, spirit, mind, and reason, setting up the full range of dichotomies we have discussed above. Also related are the emphasis on God's eternal, unchanging nature and on God as "uniquely alone." It is but a step from this to putting male (spirit/thought/creator) above female (nature/body/creation) in hierarchical fashion.

I agree with feminist theologians that we must do away with the insufferable philosophical dualism that puts women at the bottom. In fact, dualism is unnecessary if we recognize that, for us as Jews, two things are at stake: our understanding of God as totally free of limitations, absolutely free to create, and the idea that we partake of this freedom in some degree even though we, unlike God, have limitations. Since we are made in God's image, in some respect we are like God. The problem is, the part that is like God is described, in most of Western tradition, as our spirit, soul, or mind. What is left over—body, flesh, animal self—then is regarded as not like God. This is the root of the difficulty.

Having a thinking machine in our brains or an incorporeal soul residing somewhere inside does not make us like God. Rather it is in freedom of the *will,* soul freedom, that we are like God. We have the capacity to act beyond our nature, to change ourselves, to decide and act in any moment. It is often taught that the seat of the soul is in the mind or brain. This makes it sound as if the soul (and therefore the will) is primarily a thinking entity, a rationalist creation. But this is not the case. The soul is the seat of the will. The mind or brain may formulate that will into what we recognize as "thought," but it is the will that originates any decision or non-habitual action—the will that is beyond the mind.

Feminist thinkers, frustrated with the frequent masculine insistence on the primacy of thought, suggest an alternative: that the root of our will is not rational thought but feeling—feeling understood in the broadest sense as our experienced, embodied relation to the world and in the deepest sense as our intuition. Yet most Jewish moral perspectives hold that feelings are not a good guide to morality. They may be honored as signals of happiness or distress, but they are essentially selfish and must be trained and curbed in order not to run to excess. Anger, for example, is regarded in rabbinic tradition as an expression of idolatry—idolatry of the self. Love, while it may appear altruistic, is often a mask for self-love. Even positive feelings connected with religion cannot be trusted as certain guides to spiritual development. They may only tempt one into pride and self-satisfaction. In most ethical and Chassidic texts, the theme is rehearsed that one cannot trust one's feelings very far; only the revelation of Torah from God, as it has been passed on through authentic tradition, can give proper guidance.

Some feminists do recognize, in passing, the possibility of too much reliance on feelings. Harrison, while stressing the importance of feelings in our moral perceptions, also acknowledges that feelings do not necessarily lead to "wise or humane action." Catherine Keller also recognizes that the love expressed in the "almost animistic" idea of inseparability from other beings and things "is vulnerable to criticisms of solipsism, narcissism, and stagnation." Then, we may ask, where do wisdom and humanity to guide our actions come from? Are we then forced to return to the intellectualist tradition that insists on the supremacy of thought and the rejection of feelings?

Jewish tradition answers that the matter is complex: mind, body, emotion are all involved. As the sages of rabbinic times said, "The kidneys advise, the heart understands" (Berachot 61a). We could argue long over how we as human beings actually work—how our will comes to be active in the world and how our will can best be opened to the right way of action. It is possible that men and women experience this differently in the intricate intermingling of body, mind, and emotion. In any case, what we learn—and this is verified over and over again in the experience of the observant Jew—is that this complex wisdom is most fully embodied in our inherited body of tradition, mediated through the words of our teachers.

Specifically, we must insist, through the *words* of our teachers. Let us remind ourselves of the picture we are given in Genesis of God the Creator. God's distinctive characteristic—which he passes on to those made in his image—is that of Speaker, the Speaker-Who-Creates, the one who brings things into being by speaking them. This is an aspect of God's transcendence: what is not part of nature, not part of the round of birth and rebirth, of karmic or natural law. We are not told anything about God's thoughts or feelings here. Speech is the mode in which, so far as we can know, the Divine Will comes into being; it manifests God's freedom to create.

This is so for us as well. Speech has a freedom, a "transcendence" that the rest of nature does not have. Communication goes on among the rest of the creatures, but speech in the creative sense does not—or at least not without humans to help it come to voice. Yet we need not make this Creative Speech into the Greek *logos,* with its platonic associations of detached rationality. Plato regarded poetry and drama as decidedly inferior to philosophy; as a result, much of our Western philosophical heritage separated pure thought, and speech as its vehicle, from feeling, intuition, dream, vision, physicality. As Jews we can leave Plato behind and recover our own ways of speaking—in ritual, song, poetry, story, prophecy as well as reasoned discourse.

Again, the Jewish dual tradition is important: halacha—the speech of rationality and logic—and aggadah—the speech of story, dream, vision—never were entirely separated. The Talmud, our great classic compilation of oral law, mixes the two throughout. In practice the handing down of the law always should be from person to person, teacher to student, Rav to questioner—an ongoing dialogue, not merely laws read from books. Judaism has been, to borrow Plaskow's terms, "passionate, communal, embodied." But historically, as the speech of halacha became dominant, beginning with the monarchy and exile and increasing enormously in the Greco-Roman period, less came from the feminine side. Women, once visionaries and prophetesses, spoke less in the public realm as the centuries passed.

Now women are recovering, taking back their share of the power of speech. Women's midrash, women's prayers, women's inspiration are rising once again; and as women become engaged in the creative work of public speech, it will affect all of Jewish life, including halacha. This is the way to address the issue of dualism—not by philosophical arguments on behalf of the importance of feelings, but by what we speak. It will become apparent through our speech that our bodies also speak truth, that our feelings and intuitions can interact with Torah learning to provide guides to action. Speaking out is taking part in the creative act by which God continues to bring new things into the world, to act with compassion and caring, in ways beyond what we as women have done before. And we do this from the place of immanence, from our connection to the divine hiddenness, from our knowledge of the Shekhinah, of Rachel weeping with us. And we ask men to call back to their consciousness the knowledge of immanence: that they too are created bodies, they must speak from feeling, they must make their creative work in the world compassionate, related, feminine.

The feminine has much to say in Jewish tradition, and the years ahead promise stimulating dialogue between the community of women and that of men. This brings us to the final point.

Too often when we speak as feminists we set up another "we-they" dichotomy, objectifying men in our speech as they have done to us in so many ways. But if we truly live in a relational world, where each is part of the other, men are part of us too, both inwardly in our androgynous psyches and in the web of life in which we move. The universe, according to our Jewish understanding, rests on the delicate balance of male and female, one that we must work out in our families, our communities, and the public world. As I mentioned above, *Adonai echad*—God is one—does not need to mean, "God is uniquely alone." God's oneness, the divine unity, is the marriage of female and male, the transcendent union that is neither mind nor body, spirit nor matter, nor anything else we can comprehend. For us it means we seek the unity of inner knowing and soaring mind, creative speech and compassionate wisdom from within ourselves and among ourselves, in community.

Questions for Reflection on Tamar Frankiel

1. How does Frankiel think feminists have misunderstood God's transcendence, and how does she understand it? Why is it essential to Judaism not to eliminate God's transcendence?
2. How does she understand our being in the "image of God," and how does her interpretation bypass the problem of mind-body dualism?
3. The feminists she cites emphasize the fact that women's spirituality is more relational and communal than men's. How does Frankiel find these elements in Judaism? Has Frankiel convinced you that traditional Judaism does not in fact denigrate the feminine? Why or why not? What would Carol Christ or Elizabeth Johnson say in response to her arguments?
4. The New Testament uses Greek concepts to convey its message in a way the Old Testament does not, speaking for example of "the word (logos) made flesh" (John 1:14). In view of this fact, is Frankiel's interpretative strategy available to Christians as well as to Jews?

Difference Feminism and the Role of Women in the Church

CELIA WOLF-DEVINE

Feminism has historically included both women who strongly value their own distinctive virtues and are concerned about women's special needs and women who are suspicious of that whole tradition because they think that these ways of thinking hold women back and trap them in subordinate roles. In this essay, Wolf-Devine explores the "difference feminists," influenced by Carol Gilligan, and connects their thought with the debate about the role of women in the Church.

Part I: Difference versus Assimilation

Since women make up half the human race, feminism—not surprisingly—has historically included both women who strongly value their own distinctive virtues and are concerned about women's special needs, and women who are suspicious of that whole tradition because they think that these ways of thinking hold women back and trap them in subordinate roles. Instead, they minimize differences between women and men and see a just society as one in which women are not treated differently from men in any important way. Their ideal is an assimilationist one. Assimilationist feminism has, generally, been more prevalent among elite women with high career aspirations, while those who regard sexual difference as important are more often members of the working class. For example, the ERA was defeated in large part by difference feminists, and the inclusion of women under Title VII (a bill aimed at black civil rights) was opposed by blue-collar

Wolf-Devine. Written for this volume. Author permission.

women's unions because it would eliminate the women's protective legislation, for which the unions had fought hard. It was pushed through by wealthy Republican women, sometimes called the "tennis shoe ladies." Men who identify themselves as feminists tend to be assimilationists.

Assimilationist feminists are quick to label any practice that treats women and men differently as "sexist," a term originally chosen to suggest an injustice similar to racism. This term, unfortunately, is hopelessly vague. It could range all the way from laws designed to protect women (such as limiting the amount of weight a woman could be required to lift on a job), or perfectly innocent practices like a young man opening the door for his date or offering to help a woman with a heavy suitcase when he would not do so for a man, to blatant unfairness or outright misogyny. Sexual difference goes deeper than racial differences and is connected with our sexual and reproductive desires, so treating men and women differently is a practice that is not going to go away. Obviously, some reasons for treating men and women differently are defensible; some are not. One has to examine the reasons given.

In her groundbreaking work on difference feminism, *In a Different Voice: Psychological Theory and Women's Development* (1982), Carol Gilligan sought to draw attention to women's special strengths and to correct for the systematic devaluation of these by our male-dominated society. Women, she argued, should identify more positively with their own distinctive style of reasoning about ethics instead of feeling that there is something wrong with them because they do not think like men (as Kohlberg's and Freud's theories implied). Inspired by her work, feminists such as Nel Noddings, Annette Baier, and others tried to articulate further the "feminine voice" in moral reasoning. Feminists like Adrienne Rich and Sara Ruddick agreed that women have distinct virtues and argued that the virtues commonly associated with women need not be self-victimizing; when properly transformed by a feminist consciousness, women's special strengths can be productive of new social visions.

Although I'm not quite sure what is meant by "a feminist consciousness," I'm inclined to agree that the virtues and values characteristic of "the feminine voice" point toward a good new social vision that has yet to be realized, and that looking at the role of women in the Church through this lens sheds light on what is going on and what is at stake. My widely reprinted 1989 essay "Abortion and the 'Feminine Voice'" looked at abortion through this lens, concluding that those praising "feminine voice" virtues and values were inconsistent in their call for abortion on demand. Here, I look at another issue through that lens.

Part II: The "Feminine Voice"

A. Moral Reasoning

Since Gilligan's work was so influential, I begin with a quick summary of it.

According to Gilligan, girls, being brought up by mothers, identify with them, while boys must define themselves through separation from their mothers. As a result, girls have "a basis for empathy built into their primary definition of self in a way that boys do not." Thus, while masculinity is defined by separation and threatened by intimacy, femininity is defined through attachment and threatened by separation; girls come to understand themselves as embedded within a network of personal relationships.

A second difference concerns attitudes toward general rules and principles. Boys tend to play in larger groups than girls and become "increasingly fascinated with the legal elaboration of rules, and the development of fair procedures for adjudicating conflicts," as Gilligan points out. We thus find men conceiving of morality largely in terms of adjudicating fairly between the conflicting rights of self-assertive individuals. Girls play in smaller groups and accord a greater importance to relationships than to following rules. Instead of emphasizing impartiality, which is more characteristic of the masculine perspective, girls are especially sensitive to the needs of the particular other. They think of morality more in terms of having responsibility for taking care of others and place a high priority on preserving the network of relationships that makes this possible. While the masculine justice perspective requires detachment, the feminine care perspective sees detachment and separation as themselves the moral problem.

Inspired by Gilligan, many feminist philosophers discovered a masculine bias in traditional ethical theories. Nel Noddings wrote a book entitled *Caring: A Feminine Approach to Ethics and Moral Education*, and Annette Baier praises Hume (in contrast with Kant) for his emphasis on the positive role of the affections in ethics, proposing that trust be taken as the central notion for ethical theory. Christina Hoff Sommers argued for assigning a central role to special relationships in ethics. And Virginia Held has suggested that the mother-child relationship be seen as paradigmatic of human relationships, instead of the economic relationship of buyer/seller (which she sees to be the ruling paradigm now).

The "feminine voice" in ethics, then, attends to the particular other, thinks in terms of responsibilities to care for others, is sensitive to our interconnectedness, and strives to preserve relationships. It contrasts with the masculine voice, which speaks in terms of justice and rights, stresses consistency and principles, and emphasizes the autonomy of the individual and impartiality in one's dealings with others.

B. Human Nature: Mind and Body

Feminist writers have also discovered a masculine bias in the way we think of mind and body and the relationship between them. A large number of feminists, for example, regard radical mind/body dualism as a masculine way of understanding human nature. Alison Jaggar, for example, criticizes what she calls "normative dualism" for being "male biased" and defines normative dualism as "the belief that what is especially valuable about human beings is a particular 'mental' capacity, the capacity for rationality."

C. Ecofeminism: Our Place in Nature

Another critic of dualism is Rosemary Radford Ruether, a theologian. Her book *New Woman, New Earth* is an extended attack upon what she calls transcendent hierarchical dualism, which she regards as a "male ideology." By "transcendent dualism" she means the view that consciousness is "transcendent to visible nature" and that there is a sharp split between spirit and nature. In the attempt to deny our own mortality, our essential humanity is then identified with a "transcendent divine sphere beyond the matrix of coming to be and passing away." In using the term "hierarchical," she means that the mental or spiritual component is taken to be superior to the physical. Thus "the relation of spirit and body is one of repression, subjugation and mastery." Dodson Gray, whose views resemble Ruether's, poetically contrasts the feminine attitude with the masculine as follows:

> I see that life is not a line but a circle. Why do men imagine for themselves the illusory freedom of a soaring mind, so that the body of nature becomes a cage? 'Tis not true. To be human is to be circled in the cycles of nature, rooted in the processes that nurture us in life, breathing in and breathing out human life just as plants breathe in and out their photosynthesis.

Carolyn Merchant, in her book *The Death of Nature: Women, Ecology and the Scientific Revolution*, focuses on the Cartesian version of dualism as particularly disastrous to our relationship with nature, and finds the roots of our present ecological crisis to lie in the seventeenth-century Scientific Revolution—itself based on Cartesian dualism and the mechanization of nature. According to Merchant, both feminism and the ecology movement are egalitarian movements that have a vision of our interconnectedness with each other and with nature. Feminists who stress the deep affinities between feminism and the ecology movement are often called "ecofeminists." Stephanie Leland, radical feminist and co-editor of a collection of ecofeminist writing, has explained that "Ecology is universally defined as the study of the balance and interrelationship of all life on earth. The motivating force behind feminism is the expression of the feminine principle. As the essential impulse of the feminine principle is the striving toward balance and interrelationship, it follows that feminism and ecology are inextricably connected." The masculine urge is, she says, "to separate, discriminate and control," while the feminine impulse is "toward belonging, relationship and letting be."

The urge to discriminate leads, Leland says, to the need to dominate "in order to feel secure in the choice of a particular set of differences." The feminine attitude springs from a more holistic view of the human person and sees us as embedded in nature rather than standing over and above it. It entails a more egalitarian attitude, regarding the needs of other creatures as important and deserving of consideration. It seeks to "let be" rather than to control, and maintains a pervasive awareness of the interconnectedness of all things and the need to preserve this if all are to flourish. Interconnectedness, which we found to be an important theme in feminist ethics, thus reappears in the writings of the ecofeminists as one of the central aspects of the feminine attitude toward nature.

D. *Paradigms of Social Life*

Feminists' descriptions of characteristically masculine and feminine paradigms of social life center around two different focuses. Those influenced by Gilligan tend to stress the contrast between individualism (which they take to be characteristic of the masculine "justice tradition") and the view of society as "a web of relationships sustained by a process of communication" (which they take to characterize the feminine "care perspective"). According to them, the masculine paradigm sees society as a collection of self-assertive individuals seeking rules that will allow them to pursue their own goals without interfering with each other. The whole contractarian tradition from Hobbes and Locke through Rawls is thus a masculine paradigm of social life; we are only connected to others and responsible to them through our own choice to relinquish part of our autonomy in favor of the state. The feminine care perspective guides us to think about societal problems in a different way. We are already embedded in a network of relationships and must never exploit or hurt the other. We must strive to preserve those relationships as much as possible without sacrificing the integrity of the self.

The ecofeminists, pacifist feminists, and those whose starting point is a rejection of dualism, tend to focus more on the contrast between viewing social relationships in terms of hierarchy, power, and domination (the masculine paradigm) and viewing them in a more egalitarian and nonviolent manner (the feminine one). Feminists taking this position range from the moderate ones who believe that masculine social thought tends to be more hierarchical than feminine thought, to the extreme radicals who believe males are irredeemably aggressive and dominating, and prone to violence in order to preserve their domination. The more moderate characterization of masculine social thought simply says that men tend to prefer a clear structure of authority; they want to know who is in control and have a clear set of procedures or rules for resolving difficult cases.

The more extreme view, common among ecofeminists and a large number of radical feminists, is that males seek to establish and maintain patriarchy (systematic domination by males) and use violence to maintain their control. These feminists thus see an affinity between feminism (which combats male violence against women) and the pacifist movement (which does so on a more global scale). Mary Daly, for example, holds that "the rulers of patriarchy—males with power—wage an unceasing war against life itself. . . . Female energy is essentially biophilic." Another radical feminist, Sally Miller Gearhart, says that men possess the qualities of objectification, violence, and competitiveness, while women possess empathy, nurturance, and cooperation. Thus the feminine virtues must prevail if we are to survive at all, and the entire hierarchical power structure must be replaced by "horizontal patterns of relationship." Women are thus viewed by the pacifist feminists as attuned in some special way to the values and attitudes underlying a pacifist commitment. Sara Ruddick, for example, believes that maternal practice, because it involves "preservative love" and nurtures growth, involves the kinds of virtues that, when put to work in the public domain, lead us in the direction of pacifism.

Difference feminists generally do not hold that the differences we discover between men and women are only the result of biological differences or that all women necessarily manifest them. Cultural, historical, and personal variation enter in as well. None of us is 100 percent masculine voice or feminine voice; men can and do manifest some of the values and virtues characteristic of the "feminine voice." Pope Francis, for example, has looked at some issues through a more "feminine voice" lens than men commonly do. But according to the difference feminists, the virtues associated with the "feminine voice" are ones people in our culture tend to associate with women. They are more frequently to be found in women, and are to be praised wherever they are found. We need to beware, however, of the assumption that all feminine traits are good and all masculine ones are bad, as some of the radical difference feminists hold. One could easily write an essay on masculine voice virtues and feminine voice vices. It is just that in a highly competitive society such as our own, feminine virtues tend to be neglected.

Part III: Women in the Church

Looking now at the Church, the question presents itself whether the assimilationist model or the difference model is appropriate in thinking about the role of women in the institutional Church. In fact, we find elements of both. Male-female difference has no place when we speak of being baptized into Christ (Galatians 3:28) or receiving the eucharist or absolution for sins in the confessional. But certain symbolic and sacramental roles are reserved to men just as they were in Judaism (in spite of the prevalence of priestesses in the religions of their neighbors). Women could be judges and prophets but not priests offering the temple sacrifices. And Jesus has the unique role of being both priest and sacrifice. The Passover lamb had to be male, and Jesus, understood as the sacrificial lamb offering his own blood for our salvation, was appropriately male as well.

The demand that women be ordained priests often relies upon the assimilationist ideal, according to which women and men are interchangeable in principle. But if, as the difference feminists claim, women, on average (for whatever reason), are more likely to manifest certain talents and virtues, then the Church needs to find ways to draw on these for the good of all. If, for example, the ethics of care (the feminine voice in ethics) emphasizes preserving relationships and providing support for the most vulnerable, then women could contribute to doing some things badly needed right now, such as developing a genuine and welcoming community where people pray together, and reach out to help each other in need. In Christian churches with married pastors—such as the Orthodox or the Anglicans—the pastor's wife traditionally played an important role doing this sort of thing and also provided spiritual counsel especially to the women of the community. Pastoral counseling is thus another area where women's talents could be utilized.

Historically, women have always played a major role in the Catholic Church. There have been nuns who have done heroic work as teachers, nurses, abbesses, hospital directors, missionaries, founders of schools and orphanages for poor children, counselors, and caregivers for the dying (as St. Teresa of Calcutta has done so visibly in recent years). Four women have been declared Doctors of the Church, and several have served as advisors to popes.

The Roman Catholic Church currently has a program for lay pastoral assistants who report to the priest. Such positions are open to both men and women, and the Church offers training for candidates. One important role they have is directing programs for religious education in the parish generally and specific classes to prepare converts to receive the sacraments (RCIA, or Rite of Christian Initiation of Adults), but they also are trained to encourage and coordinate volunteer activity on the part of members and to find ways to draw on their talents. They could, for example, arrange rides to mass for people unable to get there on their own, or help parishioners who live alone get to a doctor or hospital in an emergency. A blind friend of mine who serves as a lector at her church recently became seriously ill and called her parish for help getting a ride to the emergency room, and the woman who answered the phone was unable to help her. In a healthy parish this would not have happened.

A Methodist church I know of has a "member care" committee, and the chair of it has a list of potential volunteers. People cannot be coerced into helping, obviously, and many have jobs and responsibilities that take up their time, but at least there is an acknowledgment that we need to care for each other and a structure set up for channeling help to those in need. A Baptist church I know of has a "Benevolent Fund" (heavily subsidized by a wealthy member) to which members may apply for help. Although enormous numbers of people live alone, the Catholic Church still tends to think that those attending mass all have large, supportive Catholic families and are ready to take on "the worldwide task of caring for the hungry and despairing," as a hymn we sometimes sing puts it. What of the hungry or despairing among us?

Priests cannot do everything needed to keep a healthy community going. In the early church, deacons were appointed to help the Apostles so they could concentrate on preaching and administering the sacraments rather than waiting on tables and providing assistance to poor widows. One suggestion for drawing on women's talents, then, is that they be appointed deacons. There is, arguably, some New Testament and historical support for this practice. There are permanent male deacons who are married and do not intend to become priests. So why not women? In part this is a prudential judgment. If the women appointed are hungry for power and treat the Diaconate merely as a stepping-stone to the priesthood, this could lead to problems. For that matter, men who aspire to Holy Orders as a path to power should be weeded out somewhere in the discernment process.

Thinking in terms of power and hierarchy represents a masculine voice way of thinking about social structures rather than the more egalitarian vision of the difference feminists, who see society more as a web of relationships. It also flies in the face of the servant priesthood envisioned by Christ who, being God, humbled Himself to become man and die for our salvation. In Catholic theology, a priest is not merely an official with a position of power in a hierarchical institution; rather, he is a symbol of Christ. Christians believe that the incarnate God suffered for our sake. Emphasis on power impoverishes the rich Christian understanding of God. Muslims have 99 names for Allah representing different dimensions of His being. Exclusive emphasis on His power distorts our understanding of who God is. Through the sacrament of Holy Orders, a priest is conformed to Jesus Himself, standing in His place, and given the authority to perform the sacraments—to hear confessions and grant absolution, and to consecrate the bread and wine at the mass, so that they become the body and blood of Christ. Thus he represents God's love and mercy at least as much as His power.

How we name God is important at a number of levels. First, there is the question of doctrine—Church teaching, grounded in Scripture and stated in the Nicene Creed, which says Jesus is God's "only begotten son" ("God from God, light from light, true God from true God" and "consubstantial with the Father"). In the Gospels, Jesus instructs His followers to address God as "Father." Jesus is the son of God and invites us into that same sort of relationship with God. But if you think about naming God only on the level of doctrine and politics (how it affects the place of women in society), something important is being left out. There is also the level of private prayer and devotion. Christians are invited to enter into a personal relationship with God, and what images we employ to think about God can affect this deeply, as Davis and Heine point out. These can vary widely between people without it being the case that the liturgy of the Christian community ought to adopt the images one person finds helpful, or avoid one that another finds upsetting. Thinking of God as personal will bring some gendered images to mind: the persons we know are male or female. And we experience God through the physical, emotional, and instinctual nature He has given us, colored by our own personal experiences. The writings of mystics and saints abound with images they have found helpful in prayer: spousal imagery, nursing at the breast of God, God as potter shaping our clay, the Holy Spirit as breath or wind or fire, and so on.

Doctrine and devotion cannot, of course, be totally separated. Jesus, incarnate God, shows us through His teachings and actions how to understand God and His intentions toward us. Some people's experiences of God have a privileged position in defining our understanding of God—for example, Moses or St. Paul. And not every image for God would be compatible with the Gospel. But Scripture and the mystical tradition abound with a rich variety of ways we may image God, and it would be a shame if believers were deprived of the freedom to follow God's leading to enter into relationship with Him in whatever way God is calling them to.

In sum, the elements of assimilation and difference combine in complex ways in the relationships between members of the Church, and in our personal and corporate patterns of imagining and naming our relationship with God, patterns that require ongoing discernment in the light of Scripture as read in the handing over of the Gospel in Tradition. Ongoing discernment, however, must not be allowed to deteriorate into a power struggle. The advantage of coming at the issue from the perspective of difference feminism is that it inspires us to think constructively about ways to draw on women's talents to build up the church. Some sort of authority structure is necessary for the survival of any institution, but thinking about this in terms of power and domination is a decidedly "masculine voice" way to think. The role of authority in the church is not to exalt its holder, but to serve the church by providing a framework for common life. Jesus contrasts the kind of servant priesthood He envisions (Matthew 20:25) with the way the great ones of the gentiles "lord it over" them and instructs the disciples instead to be the servants of all. Thinking about priestly ordination in terms of power, as most assimilationist feminists do, sets us up for a struggle conducted in the "masculine voice" language of power and rights that, if successful, would bring about a schism.

Questions for Reflection on Celia Wolf-Devine

1. The differences between women and men are both obvious to the untutored eye and supported by our knowledge of human genetics and the teaching of the Book of Genesis. How, then, can assimilationist feminists deny their importance? Are they just Nietzscheans expressing their will to power over nature and other human beings, or is there some other way of understanding their reasons?
2. To what extent is the difference between the sexes a matter of culture, and to what extent one of biology? Can we keep these two sides of ourselves separate?
3. Some people now hold that instead of two sexes, we should recognize sixty-three genders. Do you agree? How does this issue affect the argument?
4. In your view, does recognizing the difference between men and women imply female subordination? That the proper sphere of women is "children, church, and kitchen"?
5. A jingle has it that little boys are made of "snips and snails and puppy dog tails" and little girls of "sugar and spice and everything nice." Is this a fair statement of the difference feminist position?
5. In most parts of America, even the most conservative people these days accept women as political leaders. How are priests different?

FOR FURTHER READING

Adams, Carol J., ed. *Ecofeminism and the Sacred*. New York: Continuum, 1993.

Ahmad, Leila. *Women and Gender in Islam: Historical Roots of a Modern Debate*. New Haven, CT: Yale University Press, 1993.

Al-Hibri, Azizah. *Women in Islam*. London: Pergamon Press, 1982.

Aquinas, Thomas. *Summa Theologiae*. New York: Benzigner Brothers, 1948. Ia. Q. 33 (on God the Father), Q. 92. esp. a. 3 (on the Creation of Woman).

Barth, Karl. *Church Dogmatics: A Selection*. Helmut Gollweizer and G.W. Bromiley, eds., G.W. Bromiley, trans. New York: Harper Torchbooks, 1962.

Carmody, Denise Lardner. *Women and World Religions*. Nashville, TN: Abingdon, 1979.

Carr, Anne. *Transforming Grace: Christian Tradition and Women's Experience*. San Francisco: Harper & Row, 1988.

Catechism of the Catholic Church. Liguori, MO: Liguori Publications, 1994. Nos. 232–267, 2779–2785 (God as Father), Nos. 369–373 (male and female), Nos. 1601–1666, 2197–2233, 2331–2400 (sex, marriage, and family).

Coakley, Sarah. *God, Sexuality, and the Self*. Cambridge: Cambridge University Press, 2013.

Cooey, Paula, William Eakin, and Jay McDaniel. *After Patriarchy: Feminist Transformations of the World's Religions*. Maryknoll, NY: Orbis, 1991. Includes Riffat Hassan, "Muslim Women in Post-Patriarchal Islam."

Cooke, Miriam. *Opening the Gates: A Century of Arab Feminist Writing.* London: Virago, 1989.

Cuneo, Michael W. *The Smoke of Satan: Conservative and Traditionalist Dissent in Contemporary Catholicism.* New York: Oxford University Press, 1997. Esp. Chaps. 3 and 5.

Daly, Mary. *Beyond God the Father.* Boston: Beacon Press, 1973.

———. *Outercourse.* San Francisco: HarperSanFrancisco, 1992.

D'Costa, Gavin. *Sexing the Trinity: Gender, Culture, and the Divine.* London: SCM Press, 2000.

Falk, Nancy Auer, and Rita M. Gross, eds. *Unspoken Worlds: Women's Religious Lives in Non-Western Cultures.* San Francisco: Harper & Row, 1980.

Frymer-Kensky, Tikva. *In the Wake of the Goddesses: Women, Culture, and the Biblical Transformation of Pagan Myth.* New York: Free Press, 1992.

Gottlieb, Roger S., ed. *This Sacred Earth: Religion, Nature, and the Environment.* New York: Routledge, 1996.

Gross, Rita, ed. *Beyond Androcentrism: New Essays on Women and Religion.* Missoula, MT: Scholars Press, 1977.

Haddad, Yvonne, and Elison Findly. *Women, Religion, and Social Change.* Albany: State University of New York Press, 1985.

Haddad, Yvonne, and Adair Lummis. *Islamic Values in the United States: A Comparative Study.* London: Oxford University Press, 1988.

Harman, William. *The Sacred Marriage of a Hindu Goddess.* Bloomington: Indiana University Press, 1989.

Heine, Susanne. *Matriarchs, Goddesses, and Images of God: A Critique of Feminist Theology.* John Bowden, trans. Minneapolis, MN: Augsburg, 1989.

Heschel, Susannah, ed. *On Being a Jewish Feminist: A Reader.* New York: Schocken Books, 1983.

Hitchcock, Helen Hull, ed. *The Politics of Prayer.* San Francisco: Ignatius Press, 1992.

Jantzen, Grace M. *Becoming Divine: Towards a Feminist Philosophy of Religion.* Indianapolis and Bloomington: Indiana University Press, 1999.

John Paul II. Apostolic Exhortation, *Familaris Consortio* (November 22, 1981). On the family.

———. Apostolic Letter, *Mulieris Dignitatem* (August 15, 1988). On the dignity of woman.

King, Ursula, ed. *Women in the World's Religions, Past and Present.* New York: Paragon House, 1987.

Lovelock, J.E. *Gaia: A New Look at Life on Earth.* New York: Oxford University Press, 1979.

FOR FURTHER READING

Macquarrie, John. *Mary for All Christians.* Grand Rapids, MI: Eerdmans, 1990.

Mankowski, Paul. "The Necessary Failure of Inclusive Language Translations." *Thomist*, 62 (July 1998), 445–468.

Martin, Francis. *The Feminist Question: Feminist Theology in the Light of Christian Tradition.* Grand Rapids, MI: Eerdmans, 1994.

McFague, Sallie. *Models of God: Theology for an Ecological Nuclear Age.* Philadelphia: Fortress Press, 1987.

Merchant, Carolyn. *The Death of Nature: Women, Ecology, and the Scientific Revolution.* San Francisco: Harper & Row, 1980.

Mernissi, Fatima. *Beyond the Veil.* London: Al Saqi, 1985.

Miller, Pavla. *Patriarchy.* New York: Routledge, 2017.

Nolan, Michael. "What Aquinas Never Said about Women." *First Things*, no. 87 (November 1988), 11–12.

Plaskow, Judith. *Standing Again at Sinai: Judaism from a Feminist Perspective.* New York: Harper & Row, 1990.

———, and Carol Christ, eds. *Weaving the Visions: New Patterns of Feminist Spirituality.* San Francisco: Harper & Row, 1989.

Plumwood, Val. "Ecofeminism: An Overview and Discussion of Positions and Arguments." *Australasian Journal of Philosophy*, Supplement to Vol. 64 (June 1986), 120–138.

Puttick, Elizabeth, and Peter Clarke, eds. *Women as Teachers and Disciples in Traditional and New Religions.* Lampeter Dyfed, Wales, UK: Edwin Mellen Press, 1993.

Ruether, Rosemary Radford. *New Woman, New Earth: Sexist Ideologies and Human Liberation.* New York: Seabury, 1975.

———. *Sexism and God Talk.* Boston: Beacon Press, 1993.

Schindler, David L. *Heart of the World, Center of the Church.* Grand Rapids, MI: Eerdmans, 1996. Esp. Chap. 9.

Schussler Fiorenza, Elizabeth. *In Memory of Her: A Feminist Theological Reconstruction of Christian Origins.* New York: Crossroad, 1983.

Sharma, Arvind, ed. *Today's Woman in World Religions.* Albany: State University of New York Press, 1994.

Skees, Suzanne. *God among the Shakers.* New York: Hyperion, 1998. The contemporary appeal of a celibate order founded on belief in a "Father/Mother God."

Smith, Jane, ed. *Women in World Religions*. Albany: State University of New York Press, 1987.

Smith, Mark S. *The Early History of God*. San Francisco: Harper & Row, 1990.

Stone, Merlin. *When God Was a Woman*. New York: Dial Press, 1976.

Toubia, Nahid, ed. *Women in the Arab World*. London: Zed, 1988.

Vlahos, Olivia. "The Goddess That Failed." *First Things* (December 1992).

Weaver, Mary Jo, and R. Scott Appleby, eds. *Being Right: Conservative Catholics in America*. Bloomington: Indiana University Press, 1995. Esp. chaps. 7, 9, 11. Shows the importance of women, the Virgin Mary, and "pelvic" issues in one form of religious conservatism.

ABOUT THE CONTRIBUTORS

Edith Black died in March 2019. She was a freelance Roman Catholic theologian living in the San Francisco Bay area. She held a B.A. from Smith College, an M. Div. from Union Theological Seminary, and an M.A. in Ancient Near Eastern Languages and Culture from the University of California at Berkeley. She was the author of an article entitled "Why Women Can't Be Ordained Priests" that appeared in *The Homiletic and Pastoral Review*, and taught Old Testament and other courses at the Oakland Diocese School for Pastoral Ministry. She also worked at Lindsay Wildlife Museum to teach natural history in the field to elementary school children.

Carol P. Christ, Ph.D. Yale, is author of the first Goddess theology, *Rebirth of the Goddess*, *Diving Deep and Surfacing*, and coeditor of the widely used anthologies *Womanspirit Rising* and *Weaving the Visions*. She now lives in Molivos, Lesbos, Greece, and conducts tours for the Adriadne Network.

Gary Culpepper is Associate Professor of Theology at Providence College. He has published in *The Thomist, Communio*, and *Pro Ecclesia*.

Richard Davis is a speaker and trainer on health care issues. His fiction has been published in *Waves: An Anthology of New Gay Fiction*, edited by Ethan Mordden, and in the *James White Review*. He is a frequent contributor to the *Las Vegas Review-Journal, Las Vegas Pride Magazine, QVegas*, and *Lambda Literary Review*.

Mircea Eliade is one of the founding figures in the study of comparative religion and the author of numerous books, including *Images and Symbols; Myths, Dreams and Mysteries*, and *Patterns in Comparative Religions*. His best-known work is *The Sacred and the Profane*.

Tamar Frankiel has taught history of religion at Stanford, Princeton, and the University of California, Riverside. She is currently Dean of Academic Affairs and Professor of Comparative Religion at the Academy for Jewish Religion California. She is the author of *The Voice of Sarah: Feminine Spirituality and Traditional Judaism, Minding the Temple of the Soul*, and *Entering the Temple of Dreams*.

Susanne Heine is the author of *Women and Early Christianity* and *Christianity and the Goddesses*. She completed her study of Protestant theology in Bonn and Vienna with a degree in philosophy. After ecclesiastical training from 1966 to 1968, and ordination to the ministry of the Lutheran Church in Austria in 1968, she obtained a doctorate in theology with a hermeneutical work on Pauline theology in 1973, followed (1979) with a Habilitation (2nd Ph. D.) in religious education. Her work was on didactics in the New Testament.

Elizabeth A. Johnson, C.S.J., is Distinguished Professor of Theology at Fordham University in New York. She has served as president of the Catholic Theological Society of America and is the author of several books, including *Consider Jesus: Waves of Renewal in Christology* (Crossroad/Herder).

Rosemary Radford Ruether is Georgia Harkness Professor of Theology at Garrett Evangelical Seminary, Evanston, Illinois, and author of *Christianity and the Making of the Modern Family; Gaia and God: An Ecofeminist Theology of Earth Healing*, and *Sexism and God-Talk: Toward a Feminist Theology*.

Juli Loesch Wiley describes herself as a "worshiper of one God, wife of one husband, mother of two fine sons, living in East Tennessee." She has been active both in the peace movement (with Pax Christi) and the pro-life movement.

Celia Wolf-Devine is Associate Professor of Philosophy Emerita at Stonehill College. She received her B.A. from Smith College and her Ph.D. from the University of Wisconsin at Madison. She is the author of *Descartes on Seeing: Epistemology and Visual Perception and Diversity* and *Community in the Academy: Affirmative Action in Faculty Appointments*. She is co-editor with Philip Devine of *Sex and Gender: A Spectrum of Views*, and of two books on prayer: *The Heart Transformed: Prayer of Desire*, and *A New Companion to Prayer: Meeting God Where You Are*. www.celiawolfdevine.com.

INDEX

A

Adam and Eve: Adam as representing all of humanity, 103; capacity of reason, 101–102; desire to become God-like, 9, 24, 102, 103; Eve as originator of life, 104; Eve as temptress, 30; exemplifying gender roles, 4, 102, 103–105; and the Fall, 7, 103

atheism, 5, 71; and belief of God as projection, 4–5

C

calling God "Father": affected by personal experience, 72, 75, 77, 129; as faithful to Bible, x, 4, 54, 64, 70, 129; as liberating, 87; as limiting, 83; not referring to father figure, 83, 85; as reinforcing patriarchy, 6, 84; pious Jews, 70, 82–84; under criticism, ix–x, 4–6; and transcendence, 2–3, 83. *See also* masculine images of God

calling God "Mother", 74, 81, 87; implications, 2, 8. *See also* feminine images of God; Goddess

Calvinism, 95

Christianity: as favoring male images of God, 28, 38, 45, 55

Cosmic Mother. *See* Mother Earth

E

ecofeminism: hierarchical dualism, 9, 30, 98, 110–111, 116, 124–126; and mutual interdependency, 97, 98, 115; and oppressing women and nature, 6–7, 103, 111; and sustainability, 89–90, 96–98. *See also* ecology; feminism

ecology: and colonialism, 95, 96; deep, 89, 90; definition, 89; and human superiority over nature, 6, 22, 97, 102; men dominating nature, 9, 90–91; and pollution, 89, 96, 98; and stewardship, 92, 102–103. *See also* ecofeminism

empowerment of women: worshipping Great Goddess, 7, 29. *See also* feminism
Enlightenment, 71, 113
enslavement, 91, 96, 115, 116
Eucharist, 42, 58, 94, 95, 127

F

feminine images of God: ix, 40–41, 83; as bride, 51, 52, 77; as countercultural, 55; emotional, 3, 75, 117, 123; as Holy Spirit, 8, 42–44; as Immanent Mother, 52, 53, 97, 105, 113; as mother bird, ix, 42, 43, 66–67, 73; as performing maternal duties, 41, 73–74, 82, 129; as pregnant woman, 67, 73. *See also* Goddess; Mother Earth

femininity: as culturally conditioned, 41, 42, 55, 103

feminism: anti-masculine views, 60, 66, 119; assimilationist, 10, 121–122, 127, 129–130; definition, 90; desire for feminine God forced, 66, 74; difference, 10, 122, 126, 128–129; extreme radical, 90, 98, 109, 125–126; Jewish, 109, 110, 112–113; materialist, 65, 91; secular, 104; spiritual dimension, 27; theologians, 51–52, 53, 81; views of fertility over time, 79, 91, 94; as women finding voice, 109, 122, 123, 126; and women's dignity, 8, 39, 40; and women's movement, 5, 28. *See also* ecofeminism

Freudianism, 3, 4, 41; and Oedipal complex, 33

G

gender binary: as enforcing stereotypes, 38, 41–44, 66–67, 74; as reductive, 41, 87, 104–105, 119

gnosticism, 93

God: relationship with erotic, ix, 67, 77. *See also* feminine images of God; Goddess; inanimate images of God; Jesus; masculine images of God; parental images of God

Goddess: creator of arts, 31; as disastrous, 8, 56; and female power, 7, 27–30, 34; and fertility, 18, 79; and mother-daughter bond, 33–34, 123; and nature, 111, 112, 114; need to use female symbols to describe, 28–29, 33, 37, 40–41, 44; and prophetesses, 105–106, 118; rejecting sexuality, 94; representing life cycle, 30–31, 98, 112; as subordinate to Gods, 29, 110; and witchcraft, 31–32, 94, 95; as withholding love, 75, 123; women's identification with, 27, 29; and women's movement, 28, 79, 81; women's will not subordinated, 32–33. *See also* feminine images of God; Mother Earth

I

idolatry, 8, 38–39, 45, 52, 78, 117
inanimate images of God: ix, 54, 63, 67; as heretical, 76; as New Age, 65; in relation to food, 74; as King, ix, 64, 70, 81, 84; as Rock, ix, 43, 54, 67, 85–86

J

Jesus: calling God "Father", 4, 53–54, 64, 82–83, 86–88, 129; as subverting male role, 8, 57–60, 67, 129

INDEX

L

language: Christians against changing, 63, 64, 103; Christians welcoming new, 63, 83; gender-neutral in relation to God, 38, 76; God as transcending, 44, 85–87, 118; impact of non-English languages, 74; as inadequate to describe God, 4, 8, 38, 82, 95; "inclusive" as excluding male images, 63–64, 65–66, 67; as reflecting personal experience of God, 8, 64, 72, 77, 129; as shaping thought, 5, 45, 65; using feminine to describe God, 38, 40, 83, 88

Last Supper, 58–59, 68

Lord's Prayer, x, 4

M

Manichaeanism, xi

masculine images of God: all powerful, xi, 16, 71, 87; androcentric, 8, 37–38, 41, 44; as appropriate, 87, 127; authoritarian, 30, 71, 123, 125; delegitimizing women, 28; divine patriarch, 41, 70; as holding men accountable, 3, 8; as husband dominating wife, 28, 95, 103; as idolatrous, 8, 39; and mercy, 16, 70–72, 74, 115; as protecting women and children, 4, 48, 71, 77; in relation to spirit, 114; and remoteness, 2, 16, 82, 123. *See also* Sky Dweller

menstruation: connection to female power, 30; religious taboos, 30, 31

monotheism: and masculine God, 4, 30, 85. *See also specific religions*

Mother Earth, 2, 13, 17–18, 116; as Cosmic Mother, 2, 7, 18; human mother as representative of, 17–18, 30; and marriage to Sky Dweller, 2, 19; refusal to harm, 17; and self-sufficiency, 18, 51. *See also* Sky Dweller

N

naturalism, xi; and orgies, 2, 19; as religious experience, 14; and Scientific Revolution, xi

naturism, 14, 15, 92

P

paganism, xi, 6, 65, 114; as deifying sexuality, 105; and demonic power, 95; and polytheism, xi, 84

parental images of God: ix, 2, 63, 73; and authority over children, 71; as strictly metaphorical, 7, 84

patriarchy: being dismantled, 39; calling God "Father" as reinforcing, 6; and female inadequacy, 38; and female subordination, 32, 33, 126; language as tool of, 65

prayer, 16, 29, 65, 129; and addressing God, 83, 129; pagan, 65; women's, 118, 127

priesthood, 8, 60, 94; only male, 58, 103–104, 106, 127–128

R

religion: as sexual impulse, ix, 1. *See also specific religions*

S

Scientific Revolution, xi, 95–96, 124

secularism: as desacralizing sexuality, 105; and nature, 95

Sky Dweller, 2, 7, 14–16; American Christians

against, 65; marriage to Mother Earth, 2, 19. *See also* Mother Earth

symbolism: as guiding thought, 3, 16, 40, 72; as political power, 7

T

Taoism: *yang*, ix, 1; *yin*, ix, 1

Terra Mater. See Mother Earth

Trinity, 64, 82, 86–87, 105; and feminine Holy Spirit, 40

Trojan War, xi

V

Virgin Mary, 32, 66; as model for all Christians, 52; role as mother of Jesus, 10, 54, 87, 94, 106; as transcending women's carnality, 30

www.ingramcontent.com/pod-product-compliance
Lightning Source LLC
Chambersburg PA
CBHW081826300426
44116CB00014B/2502